AGENDA FOR YOUTH MINISTRY

AGENDA *for* YOUTH MINISTRY

Cultural Themes in Faith and Church

EDITED BY

Dean Borgman

and Christine Cook

First published in Great Britain in 1998 by
Triangle, SPCK, Marylebone Road, London NW1 4DU

The editors and publisher would like to thank the following for permission to reproduce material in this book:
Ephrem the Syrian: Hymns, edited by B. McGinn, 1989, Paulist Press.
'The Six Stages of Moral Judgement', table from *Moral Stages and Moralization: The Cognitive-Developmental Approach* by Lawrence Kohlberg. In *Moral Development and Behaviour: Theory, Research and Social Issues*, edited by Thomas Lickona. Copyright © 1976, Holt, Rinehart and Winston.

British Library Cataloguing-in-Publication Data
A catalogue record for this book is available from the British Library

ISBN 0-281-05152-6

Photoset by Wilmaset Ltd, Birkenhead, Wirral
Printed in Great Britain by
The Cromwell Press, Melksham, Wiltshire

CONTENTS

THE CONTRIBUTORS

John Allan
Belmont Chapel, Exeter, UK.

Dean Borgman
Professor of Youth Ministry, Gordon Conwell Seminary, South Hamilton, Massachusetts, and Tutor, Fuller Theological Seminary, Pasadena, California, USA.

Anna Chakko-George
Youth Worker and Tutor in Frameworks, Oxford Youth Works, UK.

Christine Cook
Director, Contact-Jeunes Youth Ministry, Switzerland.

Reverend Nelson Elwood Copeland, Jr
President, Christian Education Coalition for African-American Leadership, Inc., Philadelphia, Pennsylvania, USA.

Ann Dickson
Training and Development Officer, Youth Link, Northern Ireland

Steven P. Gerali
Judson College, Elgin, Illinois, USA.

Sandra Millar
Youth with a Mission, and University of Warwick, UK.

Sam Richards
Director, Oxford Youth Works, UK.

Dr Don C. Richter
Director, Youth Theology Institute, Emory University, Atlanta, Georgia, USA.

Mark H. Senter III
Associate Professor, Trinity Evangelical Divinity School, Deerfield, Illinois, USA.

Pete Ward
Archbishop of Canterbury's Adviser for Youth Ministry, Oxford, UK.

Preface

Worldwide there are many more youth workers than anyone imagines. Some are full-time staff in churches and various organizations, others part-time and most volunteer workers. Bring them together and ask them if they see their work as professional. After an initial hesitancy, they realize that they are indeed dealing with problems relating to their work on a professional level and therefore need professional resources.

Today's youth workers are asking for closer networking, more training, and relevant research for their task as professionals. Christians in youthwork understand their need to theologize about their ministry. This book takes you inside a representative group of youth ministry educators and practitioners who came together to discuss topics of significance and urgency.

As we head towards the twenty-first century, new and more difficult challenges will be facing us as we attempt to understand and relate the Gospel to youth culture and to the Church. It was exciting to see that the authors of the papers presented in this book were all taking a look at these challenges from the perspective of their own experience and field of interest.

The practitioners and educators gathered spoke to the need of most youth ministers for published material from an academic perspective for reference in a variety of fields. Our hope is that this book is also a response to that need.

We would like to thank each of the contributors for allowing us to publish their work, and for the extra labour involved in getting their copy to us. Thanks, as well, goes to Pete Ward for his creative ideas, which helped bring this book into being. Our very special thanks go to Jill Taylor, who spent countless hours getting the manuscript ready for publishing. Without her, this book would never have seen the light of day.

Christine Cook and Dean Borgman

Introduction

PETE WARD

Background

On a cold winter's day early in 1994, Chris Cook, Dean Borgman and myself found ourselves in Oxford. Over a glass of wine, we started to talk about the developing field of Christian youthwork (or youth ministry). As we talked of our interest in young people, writing, research and teaching, we began to share a dream. Chris, Dean and I had been friends for a good few years, and, coming from continental Europe, the USA and Britain, we were aware of a growing number of people working in this new field of youth ministry. Our dream (which I am sure owed a good deal to another Oxford group 'The Inklings') was to hold a gathering in Oxford for anyone interested in a more reflective or academic approach to Christian youthwork. All three of us were involved in writing and we were in touch with others who were similarly engaged. We wanted to find a place where we could read our work to each other and, in the spirit of joint enquiry and academic rigour, subject our thoughts to peer assessment. A further desire was to see a growing literature in this general area of Christian work among young people begin to take shape.

One year to the day after that first meeting, Mansfield College in Oxford played host to The First Conference on Youth Ministry. Around 70 people attended from New Zealand/Aotearoa, Australia, the USA, continental Europe and the UK (our awareness of a parallel network of Third World theologians and practitioners in youth ministry linked to the Oxford Centre for Mission Studies meant that we decided to focus primarily on the English-speaking and European context). Some of the papers from the first conference were later published in the books *Relational Youthwork* and *The Church and Youth Ministry* (P. Ward (Ed.), Lynx, 1995).

The first conference was a big success. From three friends meeting in Oxford we had suddenly found that we were part of an embryonic but growing international academic community. In January 1997, The Conference on Youth Ministry met once again at Mansfield College. The papers in this volume were selected from over 40 papers presented and discussed by 80 of the leading youth ministry academics, practitioners and researchers from the first (or one third of the) world. As a result of these two conferences, those involved in them have resolved to work towards the formation of an academic community that will meet every two years (we next meet in 1999).

The need for academic reflection on Christian approaches to work with young people has become a pressing need. In the UK, Australia, South Africa, Europe and Aotearoa/New Zealand, training for youthwork from a Christian standpoint has been developing apace with diplomas, degrees and masters degrees coming on stream. In such a climate, it is imperative that writing and research is encouraged to feed this new area of applied or practical theology. The development of a variety of types of training for Christian youthwork is a response to the need of the Christian community around the world. The increasing trend towards the appointment of full-time youth workers and the specialization of clergy in areas related to work with young people has meant that there is a groundswell of interest in this area.

Those of us involved with The Conference on Youth Ministry are committed to academic work, but always with an eye to helping the Church connect with young people in ways that are appropriate, Christian and contextual. Ours is essentially a practical theological enterprise, but we are aware that grass-roots youthwork needs to be informed and inspired by creative and positive reflection at the highest level. This book represents a response by Christians who are engaged in theological and practical reflection upon youth culture and youth ministry to the needs of the Church.

Themes and Debates

Ours is a new discipline within the theological world. The papers in this collection give evidence of the variety of concerns that could be labelled 'youth ministry'. These include a diverse range of topics: the effect of films and contemporary media on young people, the role of the Church in community conflict in Northern Ireland, the changing nature of family life, the development of identity among Asian communities in Britain, the failure of the Church to recognize and value the ministry of women, the need for young people to be theologically literate, the nature of moral reasoning and development, and the rate of cultural change from one generation to the next, as well as the nature and effectiveness of the Church's work among young people.

In dealing with these diverse areas of interest, the authors draw on a wide variety of resources and academic disciplines: cultural studies, community work, sociology, philosophy, mission studies as well as biblical studies and practical theology. Some of the authors are involved with young people on a day-to-day basis and have written in an attempt to make sense of an aspect of their work that calls for deeper reflection. Some are engaged in academic research leading to higher degrees and their papers reflect the results of their work to date. Others are currently employed as professors of youth ministry in academic institutions. Coming from a variety of backgrounds and callings, it is clear, however, that youth ministry as it is presented in these various writings is wide-ranging and interdisciplinary.

Context and culture are two of the recurring themes in this collection. Whatever the impact of a globalized youth culture and the continuing march of technologies of the media, young people live out their lives in situated localities. In assessing the relevance and importance of the insights represented by the various authors, the twin themes of a commonality of 'being young' and consuming a shared media is always to be balanced by specific community histories, Christian traditions and neighbourhood groupings. Thus the generalizations that are to be found in the work of John Allan writing on film or Mark Senter reflecting on youth ministry in the United States or Sam Richards writing about the moral development of young people need to be balanced by the studies of young people in Northern Ireland offered by Ann Dickson and the work of Anna Chakko-George on Asian girls in Oxford.

The backdrop to many of the contributions is explicitly or implicitly a Christian approach to culture. The dilemma that faces youth ministers and the wider Church is to what extent contemporary culture is a site for contextualization, a place where the Gospel can be expressed, or to what extent it is to be seen as anti-Christian and, thus, a force to be resisted. John Allan analyses the role of films in developing values and attitudes among young people. He sees films as offering alternative moral frameworks for action that are often deeply morally flawed. Film engages us at an interactive level, he argues, and it therefore affects us as we are drawn into these narratives. The role of youth ministry is to offer a critique of these moral frameworks. Dean Borgman is also ambivalent about trends in youth culture, but he also stresses the importance of those working with young people continually being engaged in a struggle not only to understand but also to locate the Gospel message in the midst of youth culture. For Borgman, youth ministry is essentially an incarnational endeavour located within, not separate from, contemporary culture.

Understanding of the cultural complexity of young people's lives is often the starting point but rarely the end point for youth ministry. Nelson Copeland is acutely aware of the problems and challenges that face young people in urban America. Writing from an African-American perspective, Copeland sees the task of youth ministry as offering a challenge to young people to make a difference. With the twin ideas of what he calls 'ethical heroism' and 'evangelistic social action' Copeland offers a model of community and personal regeneration that is rooted in the Christian Gospel. Like Copeland, Don Richter sees young people making a difference in their communities. For Richter, this difference is connected to a sense of vocation, and he has developed a method of working that is based on making academic theological thinking accessible to young people. Those who are able to reflect theologically are empowered to change the world. Like Copeland and Richter, Anna Chakko-George sees the Christian Gospel as a force for cultural transformation. In seeking to understand the cultural tensions of young Asian girls growing up in Britain, Chakko-George offers the possibility for identity resolution. This resolution comes from the transformation of creation in Christ, but is rooted in the value found in both the culture of these girls' homes and the culture that surrounds them at school.

What emerges from this collection is a picture of youth ministry that is concerned to develop models of work with young people that are culturally sensitive, but also able to challenge, inform and transform those same cultures. The starting point is a desire to engage contextually with the 'lived experience' of young people. At the same time, it is the hope, desire and expectation of Christian youth workers that young people should find in the Gospel the energy and inspiration to assert not only their identity and place in the world, but also to set about making a difference in whatever community they happen to find themselves. Youth ministry is therefore concerned with the Christian development of young people. This development – whether it takes place within the Christian community or as the result of relational contact with those outside the Church – needs to develop frameworks for action and education. In Sam Richards' contribution we see the movement towards a model moral education that is rooted in a dialogue with philosophical and theological traditions. Such reflection on the way ahead for youth ministry is foundational to an effective and informed practice of youth ministry. A similar commitment to the development of young people can be seen in the work of Don Richter.

Alongside questions of culture and cultural change and the development of young people, youth ministry is also intimately concerned with the Christian community. 'The Church' is a recurring theme in these papers. Steve Gerali points out the extent to which contemporary patterns of Church life are rooted in what he calls 'boomer' culture. A Church that has found fresh life by engaging with, and to some extent adopting, the culture of the 1980s is now faced with new generations who find Church life just as restrictive and unrewarding as their parents did. The roller coaster of cultural change presents a significant challenge to the contextually minded youth minister. As the Church loosens its moorings in the worship and expression of previous centuries, the way ahead looks extremely uncertain. For Mark Senter, however, the Church, far from being at sea, is to be seen as the rock to which we cling. The Church for Senter is likened to Garrison Keillor's community in Lake Wobegon. The Christian family, and the Church community, are to be a place of refuge and of identity in an uncertain world. Youth ministry, in its tendency to separate young people from the life of the family and the mainstream Church, however, is suspect and perhaps ultimately an outmoded endeavour, according to Senter. The way ahead is to re-embrace the Church as an alternative moral community offering a sense of place and belonging for its members.

Seen from the perspective of Northern Ireland, however, the Church as locus of community identity is far from a positive force. Ann Dickson points out that, despite pronouncements at a national level from Church leaders, all may not be as it seems in Church life in Northern Ireland. Dickson charts the role that the Churches have played in supporting the underlying dynamic of community conflict in the province. Committed to 'cross-community work', Dickson laments the reactionary nature of the Church in the two communities in Northern Ireland. The challenge of the Gospel for Dickson lies in moving beyond the identities and securities currently supplied by the Church. Sandra Millar is also deeply sceptical about the Church's ability to react to the movements associated with contemporary society. Her research into the sense of value and significance that Christian youth groups consistently fail to offer to women is a salutary reminder that all may not be well in Lake Wobegon. Richter may advocate theology as a kind of tribal initiation for young people into the tradition of the Church, but youth ministry that simply assimilates young people into a reactionary and stifling environment is far from the vision of cultural transformation offered by some of the other writers.

Youth ministry may well be a fledgling discipline, but it is a creature that has some teeth! These papers show that the critique youth ministry has to offer shines the light on contemporary culture and on the Christian community as well as on Christian youthwork itself. Perhaps this is to be expected – after all, young people are at the leading edge of many of the changes that characterize contemporary life. Youth culture is central to the development, creativity and energy of all of our societies. At the same time, it is often young people who experience the tensions, contradictions and social injustices that make life in our various continents, countries and local communities problematic and, at times, perilous. This book reflects the fact that a Christian approach to work with young people will be one that pushes at the boundaries of theological reflection, Church life and Christian discipleship. There is much here that will challenge not only youth workers, but clergy and others concerned with Christian witness.

CHAPTER 1

Professionalism and Cultural Research in Youth Ministry

DEAN BORGMAN

Introduction

As leaders committed to youth ministry, we may read the command of our Lord in this way: 'You are receiving power from the Holy Spirit to be witnesses of me in all the youth cultures of the world' (Acts 1.8, paraphrased). I use the term 'culture' because it seems important for the theological task to which these conferences are dedicated. Such theological reflection on youth involves three concepts I wish to address: professionalism, culture and research. The key question of this paper is 'why and how should we make more critical use of information about adolescence and the youth culture in our ministry these days?' The information to which I am referring has to do with changing configurations of adolescence itself, of the youth and popular cultures, and of youthwork or youth ministry itself.

First, I will state some assumptions underlying this paper. To what extent does youth ministry need behaviour science and theology? Second, we address anti-professional biases and consider a positive idea of professionalism in youth ministry. Third, because some current approaches to youth ministry are downplaying the significance of adolescence and youth culture, we next take a fresh look at this developmental stage and its social results in subcultural form. Fourth, two different directions and disciplines of youth ministry are described from inside the Church to the outside, and from outside streetwork into the Church. Youth pastors and outreach workers both need research; the place of research in youth ministry is discussed. Finally, a model of relevant research is provided with implications for youth ministry.

Assumptions Behind This Paper

1 Adolescence is a social structure as well as a stage of growth. It is the transitional age between childhood and adulthood, and it is greatly affected by expectations and influences from parents, schools and the dominant society. From biblical cultures to societies today, all girls and boys have passed from childhood to adulthood. The Bible describes Samuel and Jesus particularly as growing in wisdom and physical stature, socially and spiritually in this passage. The primary socializing systems around most children and teenagers today are family, school, media and peers. Seven-year-olds are probably influenced by those four systems in that order. By the time they are teenagers in secondary school, the order may change to peers, media, family, school.

2 The prolongation, isolation, confusion and restriction of youth are significant factors in the creation of a youth culture. To the extent the dominant culture undervalues, neglects or oppresses particular groups of teenagers, youth may form unique and sometimes oppositional subcultures. The Bible seems to imply the significance of culture in Acts 17.26–7, in the Tower of Babel story, and elsewhere.

3 Significant changes in the world and in dominant society create corresponding changes not only in the youth culture but in adolescence itself. Most who work in the youth culture or study it are impressed with the rate at which it changes. To the degree the influences on children and youth change, we may expect a change in young people and their culture – and youth ministry must change in step if it is to remain contextualized and relevant (Daniel 12.4b and 2 Timothy 3.1–5, along with various other biblical passages, warn of evil consequences from some kinds of cultural changes).

4 A common thread and general consensus in these conferences has been seeing relevant youth ministry as incarnational and relational. This emphasis reflects an understanding of youth culture as subculture. Relevant youth ministry does not just invite

youth into the adult Church; it is driven by missiological urgency to enter the various subcultures of young people today. It does so as Christ entered human culture and with the intent of relational involvement with young people on their own turf. ('The Word was made flesh and lived among us ("in our neighborhood", as The Message has it) . . . As the Father has sent me so I send you' – John 1.14a and 20.21a.)

5 There are amateur youth workers who, without training and with a disdain for planning meetings, love young people and want to serve them. Although we respect such concern for young people, we are also committed to training youth workers with the best information and principles available. While we recognize that youth ministry is the Lord's, who took simple uneducated fishermen to found the Church and can still work through the uneducated and untrained to achieve all kinds of exploits, we think striving for excellence in youth ministry calls for a dedicated sophistication. In short, our common purpose here at a conference like this is to further the professionalism of youth ministry. In contrast to Acts 4.13, which underlines the fact that the apostles were 'uneducated and ordinary persons', Ezra 7.6 describes the professional skill of a scribe or biblical scholar and 2 Peter 3.15b–18 implies that Paul was trained as a professional theologian.

Professionalism in Youth Ministry

What then, do we mean by professionalism. Much fine youthwork has, in fact, been in reaction to the condescending and irrelevant efforts of some social workers and religious leaders. Many of us became youth workers saying, 'We refuse to be 9 to 5 desk-sitters who remember clients by numbers and diagnoses'. Of course, we still resist bureaucratic and programmatic institutionalism that loses the relational touch, but, shouldn't we also want to move amateur youthwork into a more mature and professional youth ministry.

As a young youth worker many years ago, I was driven more by numbers than a deep and theological sense of our calling. When our group reached 100, we were successful. When it topped 200, we were really going places. By the time it reached 300, we were the greatest. We didn't need training, nor the wisdom of elders. We used the cult of personality and the 'key-kid' concept to build up a Saturday night movement in our church basement. With many secondary teachers and students, we had no idea there was life after high school or university. We were so committed to kids in the here and now, we thought little of what their lives and faith would look like 15 years down the road. This ministry contains many characteristics of immature and amateur youthwork. Still, whenever we see young and fervent youth workers in such a ministry, we should guard against quick judgmentalism that might write it all off. For God has brought, and still does bring, significant results from such efforts. Being professional certainly does not guarantee kingdom results, but we are striving to combine youthful spontaneity, the creativity of the Spirit and sound professional wisdom.

By 'professional' we mean youth ministry that is well thought out as well as prayed through, that is holistic rather than superficial, that considers long-term rather than just immediate results, that empowers young people rather than making celebrities of its leaders. Admittedly, it is not easy to determine what is or is not a profession in today's cultures. Traditionally, professions have played a special role in a society. They have a special responsibility for society's treasured resources, be it the life of a baby, the education of children or the reputation and freedom of a citizen. This is what doctors, teachers and lawyers do. Clergy have traditionally been considered professionals because they deal with people's souls.

What makes a group of workers professional is their specialized knowledge, which is not shared by the rest of society, their training as well as academic instruction, their acceptance of a set of professional standards and their discipline by some professional body. All of us at the conference have studied adolescence to the extent that we have become an important resource for our communities. We have all received some kind of training and have probably developed training programmes for others. We are at the point of pooling our knowledge and considering standards that should guide our fledgling profession. The designation of professional comes to us because we have a responsibility for the souls of young people. With that responsibility comes a challenge to be well informed.

Youth Culture

What knowledge do we need to be more professional? There was a time when youth ministry theory jumped from human development to biblical insights and principles of ministry. Increasingly, youth leaders are seeing their need for knowledge, not only that concerning adolescent development, but also regarding the dynamic youth culture that is the world of young people. Some very sophisticated denominational youth leaders in the US and elsewhere still act as if youth ministry is primarily a family affair in a nice church setting. Certainly, all of us are deeply committed to family and church life, but most young people are growing up in a different world – a world of friends, pop culture, sensationalized news and spicy commercials, symbolized in videos of house, jungle, rap, heavy metal and alternative music. Not all young people are getting high or having sex on the weekends, but studies show that the percentage from those nice churches who do is higher than their leaders and parents would like to admit.

Human beings must have a culture as a context in which to survive, reproduce and socialize their young – as well as for human dignity and fulfilment. It is only within human culture that personal identity and status are achieved. Cultures today make it difficult for young people to work out their identities and to achieve a sense of their status. Years of further education, experience and the paying of dues are usually expected before they are ready for adult responsibility and rewards in business or even family. Teenage sports stars are the exceptions that prove this rule – and they are still playing as big kids and often relying on rather unscrupulous agents. In fact, the average teenager would not really want the responsibilities of a banker, CEO, prime minister, pastor, bishop or even running a home right now. It may sound nice to say that young people are adults now, but that is not their reality.

Dominant culture has greatly segregated and prolonged adolescence. Young people, aided by media and advertising that cater to and prey on them, establish a culture with its own language, humour, fashions and music. This youth culture is not monolithic; it is divided into many subcultures. When the folk language (or slang), folk fashion or folk music of a particular group becomes popular enough, it is quickly exploited by the media in ways that make it mainstream, mass or pop culture rather than folk culture. Young people with a need for unique expressions of their identities may feel compelled to move towards alternative, punk or neo-punk cultures. There is, then, a constant reshaping of youth culture and special subcultures within the dominant culture, and these are the contexts of our ministries.

Two Disciplines of Youth Ministry

Pete Ward has articulated what many of us have sensed for some time: that there are really two disciplines of youth ministry, as different as the disciplines of teaching and social work. The first discipline might be described as youth pastors who work from within the Church, hoping its young people will bring in outsiders. The second could be called street workers who work from without, hoping to lead young people into the Church at some point. Within this conference there are those whose style and framework is 'inside out' and others with an 'outside in' perspective.

Both styles or disciplines need a keen knowledge of the youth culture, though perhaps for different reasons and with different emphases. The youth pastor has the greatest temptation to fall into a sense that church culture, be it ever so youthful, is the culture within which group members are really growing up, making their life commitments and being discipled. Actually, the youth group may be a kind of subculture and its internalization may be only one compartment of the busy, fragmented lives of the group's members. The values they learn from us are their church values, and these may have little to do with their school values or party values. This does not reflect a superficiality in our teaching, but the fact that hurried children are growing up to be 'patchwork selves' as teenagers.[1] If a youth pastor is with a young person two hours a week, that is 1/84 of that teenager's life. The youth pastor needs an understanding of the other compartments of a teenager's life as well as a familiarity with the whole context within which the Church's young people are being discipled. Church youth leaders ought to see beyond what is sometimes a Christian or denominational subculture to various other shades of secular subcultures influencing the members of their youth group.

In the midst of this contrast, let's remember the challenge of our task:

> Jesus said . . . : 'Follow me, and I will make you fish for people'. (Mark 1.17)
>
> Go and make disciples in all [cultures]. (Matthew 28.19a, paraphrasing nations)

The idea that teenagers are the most effective missionaries to other teens has been tried and found wanting. Various organizations in several countries have come to realize that to reach into hard-core subcultures, adult missionaries are needed. Many youth ministers see outreach as training committed teenagers to reach their friends and bring them to attractive activities, but there are many young people who just won't come to such activities. Incarnational youth ministry envisions leaders, leaving adult Christian culture to enter the subcultures of youth *without* losing their own adult identity.

The outreach worker (or street worker) is really a missionary who needs an anthropological understanding of the foreign culture in which he or she is involved. Missiology is a delicate and sensitive discipline. We must see the beauty and positive aspects of all foreign cultures before we can earn the right to be heard. We enter other cultures as learners before we can become teachers. We don't just take God to other cultures; we expect to discover God there and be surprised as we find new revelations of Jesus Christ. This is not meant to diminish the singular and unique revelation of Christ as a Jew 2000 years ago, nor the revelation of the World of God in Holy Scripture. Discovery of God in other societies has to do with the continuous and unique manifestations of grace in all cultures. No culture has a corner on God's truth, though we have to admit that Americans and Western Europeans have sometimes acted that way. The spiritualities of other peoples and the instances of common grace in particular cultures can bless and instruct us in

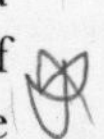

many ways if we are open to learn. On the other hand, there is in all cultures what the readings for Epiphany describe as the darkness of injustice in all cultures. Hear the cry, 'Arise, shine, for your light has come . . . all [cultures] will come to your light' (Isaiah 60.1ff., paraphrased). The evils and darkness of cultures are best judged and corrected by cultural insiders; missionaries are there to share the Good News of such hope.

Until recently, the underestimation of culture in many religious circles, and in most youth ministry books, has been a crucial vacuum needing to be filled. Without a deep understanding of culture as an idea and of cultures in particular, dynamic theologizing is limited and youth ministry is less effective.

Research and Youth Ministry

We speak of research in the broadest sense as the informational base needed for relevant and holistic youth ministry.[2] Noah Webster defines research as 'searching diligently, examining with continued care.' Another dictionary describes research as 'scholarly or scientific investigation.'[3] To occasional students who object to my wide and more popular definition, I suggest we distinguish two types of research: primary or scientific research and secondary research. Secondary research includes all careful observation, enquiry, questionnaires and surveys, and collection of news and magazine articles, as well as scholarly studies in journals. We are talking here primarily of this secondary and broader use of the term. Few of us are called to scientific research on a focused and unusually narrow aspect of adolescent behaviour or the youth culture – we applaud those who do. However, all of us are called collectively, I believe, to organize our observations and enquiries about where young people are at these days and how they may be most effectively encouraged in their growth and spiritual quests.

It seems helpful to further distinguish two types of (secondary) research in youth ministry: community research and topical research. The first enquiry of the youth worker should be a survey of his or her context for ministry. Such a survey identifies the interests, assets and needs of young people along with the needs and resources of the community. Such investigations promote critical networks that encourage holistic ministry with young people. Out of community research comes a further need for information on various issues among young people, which we call topical research. Files of clippings from local newspapers, along with national and international information, can become a resource centre for a local network of youth workers.

Examples of Broad Observations and Enquiries

Someone suggested to us that you can tell a lot about a culture if you look at what they are giving their children. So, we took a look in the giant toy stores in the early 1980s. Girls' sections were filled with sexy Barbies; the boys' with toys of violence and militarism. From there we studied children's cartoons and discovered the new product-driven stories. Not content with directing commercials at children every ten minutes, toy manufacturers created whole programmes promoting violent toys. We also began to notice three strong messages that were becoming dominant in movies, television programmes and commercials by the mid 1980s:

1 you should be wealthy and therefore successful;
2 you should be sexy and therefore popular;
3 you can be strong, dominant and violent, and therefore sexy.

To what extent do you think these three statements expressed the spirit in which US children were growing up in the 1980s? By the time 6–12-year-old children were teenagers at the end of the 1980s and the beginning of the 1990s, America was experiencing a wave of date rape and even fraternity gang rape. Are there any relationships here? Does this information suggest any implications for youth ministry?

Let's take a different look at Germany (though we are doing so now as outsiders). By the late 1970s, there were signs of spiritual revival among German young people. An understandable caution about large group rallies along with the German tendency towards bureaucratic and socially oriented youth programmes might have discouraged evangelical happenings. Instead, renewal movements and large rallies came to be not only tolerated but even supported by the German Church. Especially notable was

Kirchentag. Coordinated by the Church, this conference attracts more than 100,000 people, mostly young, each year. It is run one year by the Protestants and the next by Catholics. Themes of peace and environment are prominent, but there are also programmes aimed at personal commitment and piety with sophisticated technology and music.

In the 1980s, we were learning of a rise in neo-Nazi propaganda in Germany – including computer games that again 'sent Jews to concentration camps'. The removal of authoritarian restraints in East Germany unleashed incipient anti-semitism and xenophobia that had never completely gone away. Problems of unemployment and immigration were serious factors in such prejudice. Published reports informed the world of a growing number of skinheads and hate crimes. (Of course the American media seized on such news even though the phenomenon was probably more widespread in the US.) In response, the German legislature created remarkably strong legislation against discriminatory words and actions.

Spiritual revival also continues, however, especially among the young in Germany. Roland Werner is a young musician and evangelist who has taken over a four-day rally called Komme folge Jesus (Come Follow Jesus). Sceptics wondered how many would come to this East German town of Dresden in 1996 and how to cover its cost (which rose to $4.2 million). However, Werner's dream of 20,000 was exceeded as 32,000 young people gathered for a series of creative activities, climaxed by a rally that filled the Dresden football field. The planning group was well aware of various subcultures that would be attending – Jesus freaks, straight edge skinheads, environmentalists, those heavily into techno music and others. This knowledge helped them plan a programme with appeal and relevance for all. We need to learn from and be inspired by such models of many kinds of youth ministries around the world.

Examples of Specific Issues

Here in the UK, the Marantha Community recognized the importance of gathering and disseminating crucial facts about children and young people. In December 1993, it read a 45-page document in Parliament called 'What On Earth Are We Doing To Our Children?: An appeal to the nation's conscience by the Marantha Community'. This launched 'A Call to the Churches', sent to 3,000 Christian leaders throughout the land at the Feast of Pentecost, 1994. Here are some of the facts from this document – they are facts with which we all ought to live.

- More than 17,000,000 children in the world die each year of starvation and malnutrition (according to the United Nations).
- More than 1.5 million have been killed in wars worldwide in the past decade. Over 4 million more have been disabled, maimed, blinded and brain damaged, and more than 12 million children have lost their homes in this period (figures from Children of War – Save the Children).
- Around 750,000 British children have no contact with their fathers following the breakdown of marital relationships (figure from the Family Policies Study Centre Survey of Lone Parents).
- There are 1,300,000 lone parents bringing up children in Britain (Social Security Minister in the *Daily Mail*, 14 September 1994).
- The number of divorces in Britain has doubled since 1971 (figure from the Office of Population Consensus and Surveys).
- From 1974 to 1984, 1,626 children died of abuse or neglect in Britain (figure from the NSPCC).
- In 1993, of all the cases open to the NSPCC, 42 per cent involved children suffering or at risk of sexual abuse.
- Around 70 per cent of all adult criminals in US jails suffered childhood sexual abuse (figure from the American Justice Department Study, 1984).
- More than 250 million copies of child pornography videos are circulating worldwide (figure from *The Independent*, 19 January 1994).

The staggering implications of these statistics demand a careful consideration. What are the results of sexual and physical abuse of children? What havoc does the trauma of violence play in young lives, and how may we respond? (We present a suggested response in the form you will find in our computerized *YouthWorkers' Encyclopedia*. For information contact us by e-mail [cys@118gcts.edu] or Center for Youth Studies, 130 Essex Street, S. Hamilton, MA 01982, USA.)

Current Research on Traumatized Children

TRAUMA – an Article review
S. Brownlee: 'The biology of soul murder: fear can harm a child's brain. Living with fear puts children at high risk for problems later in life. Is it reversible?' (*US News and World Report*, 11 November 1996, pp. 71–2).

Overview This article is prefaced by a picture of two very small boys standing in rapt attention while medics treat the victim of a gunshot wound in their Houston neighbourhood. It begins with a description of three little girls at Houston's Texas Children's Hospital. Nothing about their appearance, as they sit quietly in the psychiatric clinic's plastic chairs, betrays the fact that their apartment had been raided by two armed men who tied them up, shot their older sister in the head and threatened the youngest of them (three years of age) with a gun.

Now, two days later and despite their calm appearance, their hearts are still racing at more than 100 beats a minute, their blood pressure remains high and, inside their heads, the biological chemicals of fear are actually changing their brains.

Bruce Perry, Child Psychiatrist at Baylor College of Medicine and Children's Hospital, Baylor University, Waco, Texas, is one of the researchers who is finding that trauma, neglect and physical and sexual abuse can have severe effects on a child's developing brain.

People look at kids who seem so normal after these experiences and say, 'All they need is a little love', but, actually, the results are far longer lasting.

What is being discovered are new insights into post-traumatic stress disorder (PTSD) and the nature of the human brain. Biologists once viewed the human brain as being genetically programmed. Now they are viewing it as being much more plastic or malleable, moulded by both genes and experience throughout life.

A single traumatic experience can alter an adult's brain. A horrifying battle, for instance, may induce the flashbacks, depression, and hair-trigger response of post-traumatic stress disorder. Researchers are now finding that abuse and neglect early in life can have even more devastating consequences, tangling both the chemistry and the architecture of children's brains and leaving them at risk of drug abuse, teen pregnancy and psychiatric problems later in life.

Childhood Trauma's Physiological and Emotional Effects Trauma's toll on a child's brain begins with fear. Real or imagined threats produce surges of adrenaline. Pounding heart, taut muscles and anger ready the child for the fight or flight response.

Research on neglected and abused children points to a harmful imbalance of cortisol in the brain. Megan Gunnar's research in Romanian orphanages suggests that cognitive and developmental delays correlate with irregular cortisol levels. Gunner also concluded that this damage may cause memory lapses, anxiety and an inability to control emotional outbursts.

The research of Martin Teicher (Psychiatrist at McLean Hospital, Belmont, Massachusetts, US) found fewer left-hemisphere nerve cell connections in abused children than in other children. Children with the most abnormal recordings were the most likely to be self-destructive or aggressive.

Bruce Perry's research demonstrated a variety of other disturbances in physiology, thinking and behaviour. Many had elevated resting heart rates, temperature and blood pressure. Hypervigilance is common: abused kids continually scan their surroundings for danger and over-interpret the actions of others. An innocent playground bump may be seen as a direct threat, for instance. Also, as many as 50 per cent of the children from some violent neighbourhoods show symptoms of attention deficit and hyperactivity disorder (ADHD), compared with about 6 per cent in the general population.

Children who are aroused by fear, says Perry, can't take in cognitive information. They're too busy watching the teacher for threatening gestures, and not listening to what she's saying. Frank Putnam (Child Psychiatrist at the National Institute of Mental

Health) is doing a longitudinal study (it has been going on since 1990) of sexually abused girls. He has found among these girls that, compared to those who have not been abused,

- there is more evidence of depression and suicide attempts;
- there are the initial symptoms of PTSD;
- there is a gradual decline in their IQ scores;
- they are likely to be rated not likeable by their teachers.

Remedial Possibilities Although these symptoms and the response of many teachers is not encouraging, the brain's plasticity, human resiliency (which has been the lifetime study of child psychologist, Emmy Werner, in Hawaii) and the power of loving mentoring point in a positive direction. Apparently, some children and young people are more resilient than others, but all can respond to loving care and a secure structure. Researchers now believe loving relationships can also help older children reset their response to stress when it has been derailed by abuse. This is not always easy as even a loving touch can sometimes set off a tantrum. Fortunately, researchers are also discovering drugs that can check the fight or flight response.

Failing these children and teenagers may be short-sighted, researchers like Teicher remind us. They are less likely to live up to their economic potential, and more likely to wind up in prison, on drugs or in psychiatric units. The cost to society of having a child who has gone through abuse is enormous.

Conclusion

The research and information contained in this paper are not esoteric – they should be of interest to all of us who deal with badly bruised young people or discuss such issues with young people more fortunate. They need to know what others are going through. Such information should shape our preaching and teaching. The main argument of this paper is that we need readily available information in our ministries of healing, liberation, and empowerment. The task of gathering such information should be done collaboratively. We need input from local resource centres and international organizations such as our various denominations and the Center for Youth Studies mentioned earlier.

My suggestion is that we decide what is most important for us and youth workers 'in the trenches' to know, how we can get at that information and how it can most readily be made available. By God's grace we have established the beginning of a global network, methods for gathering information, a writing guide for abstracting information, and a CD-ROM with the *YouthWorkers' Encyclopedia* and other programme and biblical resources.

Theology is best articulated by those who have a Bible in one hand and today's newspaper in the other. We need research for the theologies being presented at these conferences – and for more effective ministries wherever we labour. May all our endeavours keep clear images of young people and the youth culture in focus, and may they begin and end in the Spirit of God and our Lord Jesus Christ.

CHAPTER 2

The Three-legged Stool of Youth Ministry

MARK H. SENTER III

In Lake Wobegon, Minnesota, American humourist Garrison Keillor claims all the women are strong, all the men are good-looking and all the children are above average. Maybe that describes youth ministry at the end of the twentieth century. Strong women, good-looking men and above-average kids.

A candid look at the youth culture of this or any generation suggests that if the only young people involved with the Church are above average, a whole mission field is being missed. If the staff consists only of strong women and good-looking men, then the potential pool of leaders is dismally constricted. If such restrictions exist, it is the Church that is impoverished.

In some ways, parents and church leaders would like their youth group to resemble Lake Wobegon. After all, it is a fairly safe place to grow up – no stories about gang violence or substance abuse, no abortions and few out-of-wedlock pregnancies, no dysfunctional families (unless you consider Keillor's Sanctified Brethren as such) and few single parent homes. Yet even in the storyteller's fictitious town (which time forgot), church is more of a tradition than a vital reality and activities for youth are more of a metaphor than a redemptive force.

Yet, according to Keillor, all of the children of Lake Wobegon are above average. How could this be? Partially it is because of the collective self-perception of the local residents. They view their children as superior to the children of other communities, thus above average.

Effectively, it may be associated with a tension in which Wobegonian youth mature. On one hand, the good people of Lake Wobegon have been sceptical of progress ever since arriving in the New World from Norway. Change has been celebrated with the enthusiasm of a wake. The worldly influences of great cities like Minneapolis and St Cloud represent dangers to the time-proven traditions of their little town.

On the other hand, young people are idealistic. Keillor describes Lake Wobegon as being a hard place to live in from the age of 14 on up to whenever you recover.

> At that age, you're no sceptic but a true believer starting with the belief in yourself as a natural phenomenon never before seen on this earth and therefore incomprehensible to all others. You believe that if God were to make you a millionaire and an idol whose views on the world were eagerly sought by millions, it would be no more than what you deserved. This belief is not encouraged there.[1]

The history of youth ministry has been built around similar tensions. Adult communities distrust outside influences and, as a result, find ways to encourage the development of shared values while discouraging activities and attitudes deemed inappropriate to the younger generation. Where this has been done satisfactorily, the children grow up to be 'above average' and youth ministry has been perceived as successful.

What Makes Youth Ministry Successful?

Youth ministry is both a recent phenomenon and a classic interaction between three parties – family, faith community and a designated specialist. The difference in youth discipleship between biblical times and the professionalized approach observed at the end of the twentieth century is more a matter of contribution than of strategy or designated leadership.

The discipleship of young people has always been an interdependent function of family, faith community and a designated specialist. A three-legged stool illustrates the structural integrity of youth ministry. Each leg plays an equal but distinct role in supporting the seat, just as each of the three parties is essential for the nurture of Christian youth. As with spiritual gifts, all are essential. One cannot say to the others, 'I don't need you.' Such silliness would only cause the collapse of the stool.

Modern youth ministry is a by-product of the Industrial Revolution. Yet, even in biblical times, when the family was the accepted social unit responsible for the Christian nurture of children, the family could always find support from the other two legs of the ministry stool. The non-formal educational patterns of Deuteronomy 6, found support both from the broader Jewish community (the Sabbath and yearly festivals being the most obvious examples) and from the leaders who periodically called the community together for instruction (Deuteronomy 27; Nehemiah 8).

As society changed, the synagogue in Jewish communities, the cathedral school in Catholic parishes and the common school in Protestant denominations came into being to assist the families in their discipleship responsibilities. Rabbis, priests and teachers in turn used the text of scripture to pass values of the faith community from generation to generation. Yet the core responsibility for nurture remained with the family. As faith communities designated teachers, it was the family that ensured that children attended school or synagogue and studied their lessons. When teachers needed financial support, it was the family that bore the brunt of the tithe or tax burden.

What, then, makes youth ministry successful? I would suggest that even in Lake Wobegon, the answer lies in a balance between the three sturdy legs of the youth ministry stool – family, faith community and designated youth ministry specialist.

When a Leg of the Stool Breaks

Innovations in modern youth ministry have come when circumstances in the broader culture have isolated Church strategies of ministering to children and young people and have rendered them ineffective. Peter Berger comments:

> Through most of human history, individuals lived in worlds that were more or less unified . . . Compared with modern societies,

> most earlier ones evidenced a high degree of integration. Whatever the differences between various sectors of social life, these would 'hang together' in an order integrating meaning that included them all. The integrating was typically religious. For the individual this meant quite simply that the same integrative symbols permeated the various sectors of his everyday life.[2]

Dennis Hollinger concludes:

> All of that changed with modernity and has only intensified in our present era. The fragmentation of life which began with the division of labour in the Industrial Revolution has only increased in our information era with its service-oriented economies. The result is loss of a unifying centre to give coherence and meaning to the totality of life.[3]

Yet it is not cultural change alone that dooms youth ministry. The faith community and the family have contributed to the demise of effective discipleship by becoming attached to curricular systems, programme strategies and even leadership skills that have proved effective in a different cultural milieu.[4]

The first three innovative cycles of youth ministry since the Industrial Revolution have been focused on supporting the family in its responsibility of Christian discipleship. Sunday school, YMCA/YWCA, Christian Endeavour, Young Life and Youth for Christ have all provided a spiritual training for young people that families had failed to provide. Churches and denominations took the parachurch strategies and adapted them for the good of families within faith communities. The key to the effectiveness of these innovations has been young Christian leaders who have discovered comfortable ways to enter the world of youth and to gain a hearing for the Christian message.

Yet, buried deep behind the dynamic changes described by historians, there has been one constant factor: the faith community. Families have changed from large to small, from rural to urban and suburban, from one wage earner to two or more, from loyalty to denomination to religious consumerism, from extended family systems to blended family fragmentation. Familial changes have created a vacuum in which ministry to young people has become a refuge whereby the faith community, frequently functioning through a parental surrogate in the person of a youth ministry specialist, passes along the values of that faith community even when the family has lost the ability to do so.

As the twentieth century draws to a close, the stability of the faith community and, in a larger sense, the ethos of any type of community beyond a relationally bound set of friends, has left much of society adrift. The modernistic assumptions of progress and measurable truth have been shattered by the rejection of any concept of knowable truth or meaning in a post-modern view of the world. Common values, especially Christian values, have fragmented into individualistically driven quests for the twin goals of economic comfort (variously defined) and personal happiness. The fragmentation of community that began in Western Europe spread first to Canada and the United States, then to Eastern Europe and now is being felt in the countries of the Pacific rim. Nationalistic and tribal movements in sub-Saharan Africa and in the former Soviet block have so jeopardized personal and group safety that community is experienced as but a fleeting rest from impending doom.

In the context of community fragmentation, youth ministry finds its most serious challenge of the century. Without clearly defined and commonly held Christian values, the faith community is in danger of responding in a manner similar to the Israelites at the end of the Book of Judges when, without a king and, by implication, a coherent set of boundaries or convictions, 'everyone did as he (or she) saw fit' (Judges 21.25). Individualism will reign. Family and community will become the prostitutes of selfish desires. The three-legged stool of youth ministry will collapse with no viable alternative other than personal or, at best, group whim.

Lest the author be accused of retaining an idealized picture of the strength of the faith community, two observations should be made. First, throughout church history, the faith community has proven to be amazingly resilient. When its core manifestation became corrupt or drifted from historic orthodoxy, movements of protestation resulted and, with them, new forms of education and discipleship.[5] Today these movements might be called parachurch, yet, in reality, they are led by people who are within rather than alongside the Church. Thus the faith community, with all its faults, remains self-correcting.

Second, in many situations, the faith community and the broader community are nearly indistinguishable in their core values. Where the culture has been formed by people who share a Christian world view, the Christian consensus extends far beyond the Church itself. Young people may not obey the ten commandments or affirm the royal law of love, but they do not question their validity. In this context, the broader community has given birth to agencies that supported the family and assisted in the process of passing values from generation to generation.[6]

As youth ministry approaches the end of the twentieth century, it does so with James Dobson challenging the Church to 'focus on the family', while Mark DeVries calls for family-based youth ministry, but with very little help locally from either the faith community or the broader culture to model or even define what 'a family', much less 'a Christian family' looks like.

Learning Disabilities

In responding to the deterioration of the family, youth ministry specialists have fallen into what Peter M. Senge calls 'learning disabilities'. Though all seven of his disabilities apply to youth ministry at the end of the twentieth century, one is especially important – the delusion of learning from experience.[7] Senge points out that all of our actions have consequences beyond our learning horizon and, as a result, it becomes impossible to learn from direct experience. This is not to say that the actions are inappropriate, just incomplete. It is the unintended consequences that lie over the learning horizon of even the most experienced youth minister that must be examined by the youth ministry fraternity.

Take, for example, the case of the 'master teacher' in youth ministry. Because the youth minister was the best communicator and had a reasonable knowledge of Scripture, most of the teaching responsibilities were turned over to him or her. The young people loved it. No more dull talks from sincere but boring lay leaders. In fact, the response was so good that the youth group increased in size, thus motivating the youth leader to become even more efficient in communicating in a manner with which adolescent fans could identify. Storytelling became the norm. Soon, however, the story was not so much '*The* story' as 'my story' or, even worse, 'a good story'.

The consequences that lay beyond the youth leader's horizons, however, were two-fold. On the one hand, young people learned to be spectators, not participants, in discovering God's thoughts. They grew up 'eating fish' but seldom learning 'how to fish' or even that 'fishing is important'. Those young people are now adults and what was once considered biblical ignorance is now accepted as normal within communities of faith. The foundation from which a Christian critique of society's norms can be provided is less available to the Church than it ever has been. Like the frog that will remain in a kettle while the temperature of the water slowly rises to boiling point, Christians have become conditioned to accept that which will ultimately prove fatal.

While young people have been attuned to a 'master teacher', parents and less gifted lay leaders have been castrated from their nurturing responsibilities. A performance mentality has provided a barrier to the network of disciplers that could have been used to help young people walk with God. Instead of being communities of learners, faith communities became products of a flawed educational model of discipleship.

Another illustration of Senge's 'delusion of learning from experience' may be the cardinal principle of modern youth ministry – relational youth ministry. Though warm relationships between adult and adolescent have always been essential to healthy youth ministry, the context in which relationships are built have changed dramatically in the past 50 years.

In the context in which Jim Rayburn and the early Young Life leaders identified incarnational youth ministry, the faith community shared a common conviction that Truth was knowable (even if unknown to most unchurched young people). Loving relationships with students when developed by youth workers were viewed in contrast with the selfishness of human nature. Sin, though laughed at by students, was understood to be wrong. Social authority, though challenged by adolescent folly, was respected. Consequences, though tested via risky behaviour, were expected to be faced. In this milieu, 'relational' and 'theology' were easily connected.

Through the latter half of the twentieth century, relational youth ministry has played different roles in youth ministry. In contexts where the faith community and club programmes gave definition (sometimes very distorted) to what it meant to be a Christian, contact work earned youth workers the right to be heard by high school students. As youth group activities faced competition from a plethora of entertainment options, small clusters of friends came to define their own norms within the high school society, while the social standards of Church and campus became indistinguishable. In response to this new milieu, the beacon of Christian truth came to be the loving life lived by campus workers and those they had nurtured.

What is 'out of sight' in the latter scenario is the void that is created when the youth worker and the peer group created by that person's network of relationships are no longer on the scene. Once adolescents leave the high school ministry in order to gain further education or enter the work force, their faith community, which was synonymous with their Christian peer group, dissolves. Unless the Christian adult has built bridges from the broader faith community and Christian families to individual students, the likelihood of sustained spiritual growth and discipleship is minimal. Students fail to bond with new Christian peer groups. Established faith communities are so busy nurturing their own members that fickle young adults are seldom courted for inclusion. Young disciples are left to their own initiatives. Some survive; most do not. Few youth ministers have the physical or emotional capacity to spend the rest of their lives maintaining nurturing relationships with the ever-increasing number of young people they point towards Christ. The 'out of sight' result of relational youth ministry without rootedness in families and faith communities is a type of spiritual orphan.

Community Builders

So what is the task of youth ministry in a post-modern world? Building intergenerational faith communities that clarify biblical values and build continuity in an age of discontinuity. Communities provide models of Christian living and shelters from the self-defining values made popular in the youth culture from James Dean (*Rebel Without a Cause*) to Dennis Rodman (*As Bad as I Wanta Be*). Despite the protestations of misguided family advocates, it does, in fact, take a village to raise a child.

Peter L. Benson and the Search Institute have identified 40 developmental assets essential to adolescent development.[8] Of these, 20 assets are internal to the young person. The other 20 are external to the adolescent and reside primarily in family and community. Though Benson does not make the 40 assets necessary conditions for spiritual development, they do provide a useful template against which to examine the building of faith communities in the twenty-first century.

In order to discover the roles of family and community, the external assets can be divided in an imprecise manner, allowing for overlapping of assets from the family designation into the functions of the broader community. This division, created by the author, might provide the basis for youth ministers to understand how they can focus their efforts in supporting families and building the faith community.

Of the external assets, nine describe a family environment. These are:

1 family support – high levels of love and support;
2 positive family communication – positive communication and ensuring that the young person is willing to seek parent(s)'s advice and counsel;
6 parental involvement in school;
10 safety – at home, in school and in the neighbourhood;
11 family boundaries – clear family rules and consequences; monitoring of the young person's whereabouts;
12 adult role models – parents as well as other adults;
16 high expectations – parents' and teachers';
17 creative activities – youth spends three or more hours per week in lessons or practice of music, theatre or other arts;
20 time at home – spends time out with friends 'with nothing special to do' two or fewer nights per week.

The other 11 assets focus on activities within a broader community. These are:

3 other adult relationships – support received from three or more non-parent adults;
4 caring neighbourhood – experiences caring neighbours;
5 caring school climate – school provides a caring, encouraging environment;
7 community values youth – perceives adults in the community value their youth;
8 youth as resources – youth are given useful roles in the community;
9 service to others – young person serves in the community one or more hours per week;
12 school boundaries – school provides clear rules and consequences;
13 neighbourhood boundaries – neighbours take responsibility for monitoring young people's behaviour;
15 positive peer influence – best friend's model is one of responsible behaviour;
18 attends youth programmes – spends three or more hours per week in sports, clubs or community organizations;
19 part of the religious community – spends one or more hours per week in activities at a religious institution.

If these assets were placed within the framework of the descriptions of the Acts 2 Church, most could fit appropriately, given the cultural differences between the oppressed Church of the first century and the cultural diversity of churches in the complicated world of today. Paul's admonitions to the Ephesian Church to 'make every effort to keep the unity of the Spirit through the bond of peace' (Ephesians 4.3) may provide further theological definition of Benson's assets. Chapters 4 to 6 offer a wonderful description of the faith community in a diversity of relationships. Though personal affiliations are portrayed, the end result sought by the Apostle is a body of believers serving each other 'so that the body of Christ may be built up until we all reach unity in faith and in the knowledge of the Son of God and become mature, attaining to the whole measure of the fullness of Christ' (Ephesians 4.13).

Community-building for youth ministry in the twenty-first century will mean creating vibrant faith communities that can nurture its families and youth. The idea of community demands continuity, not just from this point onwards, but also connecting with the faith community of previous generations. While oral communication is essential for mission and fellowship, written resources, including Scripture and the resulting theological and contemplative literature, are the primary sources of continuity in this post-modern world.

The faith community must have integrity before a sceptical or apathetic audience. Faith must be lived over the long haul. Our youth needs models of Christian living who will remain in their lives for decades, not just days or even years. Symbols are needed to visualize the truth of Scripture. Art, drama, music and media must become interpretative tools for the written Word as well as the lived Word present in the Body of Christ, the Church. Celebration will be the gathering of believers, and yet integrity requires appropriate discipline, both personally and corporately. Then, at the heart of the richness of the faith community will stand Scripture as the primary constant that the Spirit of God uses to mould the witnessing community of faith.

No longer can youth ministry afford to be ghettoized as a by-product of modernity, assuming that the family and faith community legs of the youth ministry stool will support the weight of rapidly changing adolescent needs. Youth ministry in the twenty-first century must include intentional activity to build up the faith community and the family so that the rising generation will have safe places to explore its identity and discover the God-Man.

Where is Lake Wobegon Anyway?

Lake Wobegon – the little town that 'time forgot', is a product of Garrison Keillor's fertile imagination. It is a mix of life, interpretation and fantasy. The genius of great storytellers is that members of the audience identify with the episodes that overlap with their own experiences. A shared perception of the world provides the basis for communication. So it is with much of what we have come to call youth ministry. While the adolescent's world remained somewhat static, the component parts of youth ministry did not need to change – communication happened; ministry resulted.

With the fragmentation of modernism into post-modern interpretations of life and reality, Lake Wobegon is nothing more than a metaphor. Youth ministry is splintering into multiple realities, each shared by a distinct set of common experiences. Oxford Youth Works is distinct from the Oasis Trust, which in turn is different from the Stopsley Baptist Church. Guatemalan-American and Cuban-American youth are separated despite a common tongue within a relatively small section of Miami. Jocks and skaters share the same space but not the same world in a suburban high school. In most cases tolerance reigns. Community has died. Lake Wobegon has vanished. Perhaps it never existed.

The challenge of youth ministry in the twenty-first century is to start all over, not as youth ministers but as ministers; not fighting for scarce budget funding, but for survival as a faith community; not as a profession, but as prophets in a world without the Son.

> He was in the world and though the world was made through him, the world did not recognize him. He came to that which was his own, but his own did not receive him. Yet to all who receive him, to those who believed in his name, he gave the right to become children of God – children born not of natural descent, nor of human decision or a husband's will, but born of God. (John 1.10–13)

CHAPTER 3

The Reshaping of Adolescence in the Twenty-first Century and Its Effect on Global Youth Ministry

STEVEN P. GERALI

Introduction

Only in the last century has there been the emergence of an adolescent subculture by name. Prior to the 1900s, the specific needs of teenagers were becoming of more concern to adults. The formation of the YMCA in 1844 and the first American Public High School in 1875 were evidencing the beginning ground swell of concern for this specific population. Just short of the turn of the century, developmental psychologists began to label a group of people as adolescents – a term coined by G. Stanley Hall, the noted 'father of adolescence'. Hall's contribution to the social sciences was the identification of the unique developmental changes and life issues that a human being undertakes during that individual's teenage years. This opened the doors for more developmental theorists – the likes of Piaget, Kohlberg, Eriksen, Havighurst and Fowler – to contribute to our knowledge of adolescents. In the last century, we have increased our learning of teenagers; from their cognitive processes to the formation of their faith.

The last century has also given us the formation of organized youth ministry. With the birth of an adolescent subculture came the need for the Church to respond to this people group. The end of the 1800s and beginning of the 1900s noted a grass-roots movement to specifically reach teenagers for Christ. This movement took the forms of the Young People's Society for

Christian Endeavour, founded by Francis Clark in 1881, the Boys' Brigade, founded by William Smith in 1883, and the Miracle Book Clubs, founded by Evelyn McClusky in 1933.[1] Many Church denominations followed suit by offering youth specific programmes, but it wasn't until the last 50 or 60 years that we have seen the formation of professional parachurch and Church youth ministries.[2]

One can surmise that the field of adolescence is relatively new and, more specifically, the field of professional Church youthwork is in its early growth stages. In the last half of this century, we have seen the 'legitimizing' of adolescent-specific professions. Professionals with expertise in the area of adolescence have emerged in the disciplines of business and marketing, education, mental health, medicine, social work and religion. Adolescence has become a focus of research. We can continue to make great strides in our attempts to know and reach this subculture by networking with the other disciplines that are attempting to do the same. Although the last half of this century has birthed the professional youth worker, we enter into the next millennium with better skills, greater knowledge and new concerns about reaching and ministering to adolescents.

The Church Growth Movement and Adolescents

Paralleling the growth of professional Church youth ministry is the phenomenon of the Church Growth Movement. Many churches throughout the world have experienced an overwhelming growth in numbers. Western culture churches have begun to adopt techniques to keep this movement alive. The Church has become a contemporary Church that employs everything from marketing techniques to popular musical forms, drama and media in worship and the formation of small group ministries. All of this has been effective in reaching a generation of people that the world has labelled baby boomers. Baby boomers are people who were born in the 1940s and 1950s. They were adolescents in the 1960s and 1970s when youth ministry was beginning to peak in its professional formation.

The generation that followed the baby boomer one has been labelled generation X or baby busters. This generation was born in the 1960s and 1970s and came of age in the 1980s and 1990s. It has been argued that the contemporary Church growth movement is built on baby boomer generational values that alienated the baby buster generation.[3] To the baby buster, the contemporary Church is a traditional Church because (at least in most of the United States) they have never known anything other than that experience of the Church.

The ecclesiastical problem that Christendom faces is that the Church has always been slow, and resistant, to change. Thus, the contemporary Church is still a new phenomenon to much of the Christian world. There is still much resistance to the changes that the contemporary Church growth movement would have the traditional church make. As a result, we are losing a generation of people (baby busters) because of the torpid process of growth. Simply put, on the one hand we have a large portion of the Christian world engulfed in a contemporary Church setting (making this a traditional Church to a younger generation) while the rest of the Christian world is still attempting to follow suit.

Youth ministers are faced with the difficult task of keeping a pulse on the ever-changing subculture of adolescence and its relation to the Church. While the Church is processing this contemporary thing, youth ministry must remain on the cutting edge in order to be effective. Having worked with generation Xers puts the youth worker at an advantage in understanding the direction that youth ministry must go in order to reach the next generation of adolescents. The focus of attention must shift from generation X to the generation that follows.

The Millennial Generation

Beginning with the year 2000, youth ministry will see a new generation of adolescents. They are labelled the millennial generation. The millennial generation is comprised of children born in the 1980s and 1990s to baby boomer and baby buster parents. This generation will hit their adolescence, or come of age, post the year 2000. It is a generation that is wanted, precious, planned for and protected.[4] One can detect this value from the box office hit movies that Hollywood produced in the late 1980s. Movies like *Baby Boom*,

Three Men and a Baby, *She's Having a Baby* and so on made having children a high value. In the years that followed, Hollywood produced an abundance of 'G'-rated (US classification meaning suitable for a general audience) films for children. Spearheading this movement was Disney Studios with films like *The Little Mermaid*, *Aladdin*, *The Lion King* and so on. They also campaigned to re-release on video old 'G'-rated classics that baby boomer parents once knew: *Cinderella*, *Snow White*, *Pinocchio*. This created the momentum that started to move a society from what the Germans call *Kinderfeindlichkeit* (a society hostile towards children) to a society that valued children and held them in high regard.[5]

The protection of these children is demonstrated in everything from legislation to education. Children's rights are hailed internationally; crimes and abuse against children are met with greater disdain and consequence; relief programmes for children are at the centre of major charities; preventive education concerning everything from profanity to AIDS is on the rise; and there has even been a surge of child-safety devices that have flooded the market, from drawer latches to kiddie bicycle helmets.[6] This desire to protect the millennial generation may evidence itself in an overprotectiveness. Youth ministry may become harder in that the legalities and precautions incurred in producing events for adolescents may not allow these events to occur. In addition, this generation may become 'untouchable' due to the suspicions of parents and the litigation hunger of the Western world.

Family and the Reshaping of Adolescence

W. Strauss and N. Howe[7] claim that the millennial generation will be shaped largely as a result of a reaction to how generation Xers turned out and were raised. Whereas generation Xers were raised in an era when children were not valued, 'first-wave millennials are riding a powerful crest of protective concern, dating back to the early 1980s, over the American childhood environment'.[8] Western culture has become more aware of the negative effects of divorce, diversified family lifestyles, value-neutral education, throwaway and latchkey households. Strauss and Howe state:

> In contrast to 13ers [generation X] – and despite their small number per family – millennial babies frequently arrive to parents who want them desperately. The abortion rate peaked in 1980 and has since shown a gradual decline. Infertility treatment and 'preemie' (premature infant) care have become two of the fastest growing fields in medicine.[9]

Even generation X parents share this wanting and protective attitude towards their millennial generation children. This may be largely due to their reaction to their own negative upbringing. Blau describes their parenting style as 'conservative, caring, committed and fiercely protective'.[10] Many generation Xers (more than 40 per cent) saw their parents' marriages fail. They desire and are more committed to intact marriages and closer family relationships. To the generation Xer, relationships define their success in life, as opposed to upward mobility, financial accolades or career status, which gave baby boomers an identity of being successful.[11] N. Howe and B. Strauss predict that divorce and infidelity will decline among generation Xers.[12] This will make their homes much more stable and their children will not live under the widespread threat of family devastation like they did.

The future of youth ministry will need to reflect these relational values. Youth ministry will also become more prominent in the Church as a priority ministry, being less programmatic and much more relational. For many adolescents, a youth ministry will provide a family or be an extension of the family that they may or may not have. G. Celente stated that in the twenty-first century the word 'family' will broaden beyond bloodlines to include friends and neighbours who 'share values, goals, responsibilities and a long-term commitment to one another and their communities'.[13] Parents and grandparents will become more strategic in the leadership of youth ministry programmes, giving youth ministry a multigenerational perspective. This trend is already being manifested in the fact that extended families are living together because of financial reasons. Grandparents are becoming more prominent caregivers and educators of millennial children as their parents are working. They are, as Celente puts it, 'the modern equivalent of tribal elders who were valued and revered in traditional hunter–gatherer societies for their wisdom and experience'.[14] Many churches in the United States have begun to seek out professionals to oversee youth and family ministries in their churches.

The children of the millennial generation will not know the rigid gender role restrictions that past generations have known. They will see fathers and mothers in a partnership of nurture and career. Men will not necessarily be the primary source of family income nor will women necessarily be the primary caregivers to children. The notion of *quality* of time versus *quantity* of time with children will largely become archaic. This generation is being raised with the value of quality *and* quantity of time. Family is superseding career.

More workplaces are buying into the value that their employees need to be with family. This is also giving credence to the revival of family-owned businesses. Smaller, more personable businesses, will supersede the large corporations. Celente believes that there will be an antimonopoly mentality that will prevail. This will also redefine the values of a capitalistic society. No longer will the acquiring of wealth be a primary life value. 'Voluntary simplicity, once merely a counterculture ideal, will finally become a way of life in the twenty-first century'.[15]

The implications that this creates for global youth ministry is that there will be a downsizing mentality. Large numbers and large events will not measure the success of a ministry. Adolescents will want smaller, long-term, stable, relational youth ministries. The blurring of gender roles will also give rise to more women in key leadership positions in youth ministry. We are starting to see this trend realized in the fact that many churches and parachurch organizations are looking for a male and female leadership team to head their ministries. Some of this may evidence the precautions of having like gender ministering to like gender.[16] None the less, women will take a more dominant role.

Multicultural Diversity: the Making of a 'World Culture'

Baby boomers take pride in being politically correct and generation Xers glory in their ability to embrace cultural, ethnic and gender diversity. These become the backdrop for a millennial generation's perspective of the world. This generation will begin to know a world culture: they are bombarded with media images from all around the globe, they have instant entertainment of events broadcast from any country, rock stars, athletics heros and Hollywood celebrities carry a global pop culture anywhere in the world by means of satellite broadcasts, international film festivals and world tours. There seems to be more of a pervasive value to blur cultural boundaries than to keep them rigidly defined.

The rise in gang activity in the United States is no longer restricted to ethnic, socio-economic or demographic (urban) settings. In the 1990s, adolescents from the most affluent communities to the inner city have turned to gangs as their primary support system. The gang, once restricted to urban, impoverished, ethnic communities, has now become widespread and all-inclusive. This phenomenon illustrates the blurring of culture in that solutions to life problems (although ill-conceived) are no longer restricted to a certain culture.

Other factors – including the accessibility of advanced technology to the Third World, the fall of Communism and Asian economic dominance – have contributed to the formation of a world culture. W. Laqueur states that in the 1990s it was accepted that the Third World had disintegrated mainly because of economic success.[17] Advances in, and accessibility of, technology have also made this Third World somewhat obsolete. In addition, the fall of Communism and the radical embracing of capitalism contributed to the blurring of cultural distinctions. The end of the Cold War allowed a blending of capitalistic ideology with the failed fragments of Communistic thought in newly formed and liberated nations. Also, it has become more and more difficult to distinguish Eastern from Western culture. Asian economic dominance has contributed to the formation of a world culture. With economic dominance comes the propagation and blending of values. Western adolescents are experiencing Japanimation (animation Eastern-style), along with a surge in martial arts and Eastern philosophies, while Eastern adolescents experience rock 'n' roll over pizza and a coke. Fashion, music, media and ideologies have become less and less distinctive and more and more global.

The new buzzword is multiculturalism. The fields of education, social sciences,[18] business[19] and religion are concerned with a multicultural approach to their discipline. One can begin to speculate that multiculturalism may be becoming a world culture.

Youth ministry – once limited to middle-class, semi-affluent Anglo-suburban populations – will no longer be the norm. Youth ministry, to millennial adolescents, will taste of ethnic, demographic, socio-economic and multicultural diversity. New frontiers in global missions will open up to youth ministers.

Cybernetics and Virtual Technologies

The millennial generation will never know life without cable network television, digitally mastered, stereo surround sound, high-density videos, compact discs; CD-ROM computers and the Internet or Worldwide Web information superhighway. These were all in existence before millennials were. At the same time the millennial generation was born, virtual reality along with virtual technologies was coming into existence. By the time millennial adolescents come of age, cybernetics, virtual reality and virtual environments will be reaching an all-time peak.

Cybernetics is the study of communication and control processes often used to indicate a conceptual connection to, or controlled by, computers. Virtual reality is that sense of place and being that exists in cyberspace.[20] The millennial generation will be cyber-literate. It will have access to information at the touch of a button. Its reach will extend internationally. This will make the millennial generation more globally aware as well as contribute to the advancement of a global culture discussed earlier.

In researching for this paper, I went on-line to access information about virtual reality. The search produced over 33,000 hits. The implications for education can be mind-boggling. Students will have access to a plethora of information, much of which is not authoritative or virtuous. As of yet there are no concrete restrictions on what is put on the Internet. Adolescents can have access to everything from quantum physics to hard core pornography. Being on-line also gives the adolescent access to other people who are on-line. Chat rooms and e-mail will be a common mode of communication. In a chat room, adolescents can take on the personas of anyone they wish to. Conversely, these same adolescents may not be conversing with the same person they perceive that person to be. Age, gender, sexual preference, political and ethnic background, economic status and so on are all relative in a chat room. Schwartz notes that an individual can '. . . confide in sympathetic strangers with the confidence of complete anonymity'. You can question things that you've been taught without being treated like a flake. You can hear views from people that you'd otherwise never meet, people outside your geographical location, involved in jobs or hobbies that you've never heard of.[21]

Chat rooms can create a false sense of intimacy. Conversations can be intimate but extremely deceptive. The phenomenon that occurs is intimacy without contact or face-to-face relationship. To the millennial generation, the chat room may be a place to hide, but it will also be a place where anyone can vie for another individual's mind. This will be a virtual battleground. The implications for youth ministry can be great. Youth ministry will go on the Internet. Youth ministers will have an international audience that desires to be there. They will need to be better trained theologically to handle the frank, anonymous questions that they may encounter. On-line evangelism, discipleship, accountability, liability, follow-up and so on will be issues that the on-line youth minister will have to contend with.

Another cyberexperience that the millennial generation will experience is virtual reality. Os Guinness states:

> Technically, 'virtual reality' signifies an event or experience that is real in effect but not in fact. Virtual reality, in other words, is a humanly constructed technological world that combines two things: a high degree of realism in simulation and a high degree of interaction that amounts to total immersion. The term 'virtual reality' was chosen by its inventors – and avoided by its critics – because of its powerful metaphysical promise. Virtual reality is the Holy Grail of the creative power of technology.[22]

The line between that which is real and that which is virtual may become obscure to millennial adolescents as well as to those beyond that generation (due to more advanced technologies in the area of virtual reality). Scepticism may rise, addictions to virtual reality as a means of escape most likely will increase, as well as the possibility of social ineptitude. H. Rheingold is quick to agree that the potential for trance, intoxication, ecstasy and mind control is inherent in any technology that strongly affects human perceptions. He continues to say that it is speculative, at best, to draw conclusions.[23] The millennial generation will be able to experience telepresence or the ability to act and interact in a distant environment via cybernetic technology. Telepresence is the electronic analogue to an out-of-body experience.[24]

Virtual reality will also allow the millennial generation to experience cybersex. With advancements in virtual reality and the experience of teledildonics an individual can have sex without a partner. Teledildonics enables an individual to enter a virtual environment where sexual pleasure awaits. The individual wears a suit that gives tactile feedback or sensations applied to the skin, typically in response to contact or other actions in the virtual world. Rheingold describes teledildonics as such:

> You can reach out your virtual hand, pick up a virtual block, and by running your fingers over the object, feel the surfaces and the edges, by means of the effectors that exert counterforces against your skin. The counterforces correspond to the kinds of forces you would encounter when handling a non-virtual object of the specified weight, shape and texture. You can turn your cheek over (virtual) satin, and feel the difference when you encounter (virtual) flesh. Or you can gently squeeze something soft and pliable and feel it stiffen under your touch.[25]

Virtual reality will allow sex without contact. An individual can invent a partner or have another partner enter the virtual environment. This scenario was played out in the movie *Demolition Man.* This is the new world's version of safe sex – sex without contact; sex without a partner. The question of morality will be central to this issue. Youth ministers will have to deal with this issue in the twenty-first century, even though in the last 600 years the Church could not give conclusive answers to the issue of masturbation. Like masturbation, cybersex may become a quasi-dirty issue that is swept under the rug.

Post-modernism

The millennial generation will be the first generation to grow up under the umbrella of post-modernism. Although the term 'post-modernism' originated in the 1930s to categorize a form of art and architecture, it became more of a philosophy of living or a cultural phenomenon in the 1970s and 1980s.[26] To explain the tenets of post-modernism would consume volumes, so, for practical reasons, we can oversimplify the core of post-modernism to mean that truth is relative. Post-modernism contends that because all knowledge is language-bound, truth is forever arbitrary.[27] P. Rosenau proposes that the post-modernist re-conceptualizes truth as local, personal and community-specific. S. Grenz states:

> The post-modern mind no longer accepts the Enlightenment belief that knowledge is objective. Knowledge cannot be merely objective, because the post-modern model of the world does not see the universe as mechanistic and dualistic, but historical, relational and personal. The world is not simply an object given that it is 'out there' waiting to be discovered and known. Instead it is relative, indeterminate and participatory.[28]

Targeted by post-modernity, the millennial generation will become much more embracing of New Age thoughts and religions that propose that authority lies in experience. An individual's experience has just as much authority as something that is scientifically verified. Z. Bauman states that 'in a cacophony of moral voices, none of which is likely to silence the others, the individuals are thrown back on their own subjectivity as the only ultimate ethical authority'.[29] All world views, be they political, social or religious, are held suspect by post-modernism. Rosenau claims that post-modernism reduces Marxism, Christianity, Fascism, Stalinism, capitalism, liberal democracy, secular humanism, feminism, Islam and modern science to the same order and dismisses them all as logocentric, transcendental totalizing meta-narratives that anticipate all questions and provide predetermined answers.[30] R. A. Shweder would also include witchcraft, astrology, primitive cults and so on in that list.[31] Pessimistically, this leads one to the conclusion that nothing is true, yet Celente describes the millennial generation as much more optimistic.[32] Laqueur describes the optimistic certainties that emerge from the belief that 'nothing is true' as then being that 'everything is true', at least to some extent.[33]

Youth ministry to the post-modern millennial generation will become 'holistic'. It must be rational as well as embracing of the non-rational element of God. It will be logical and experiential. Grenz puts it directly:

> A post-modern evangelical theology dare not become anti-intellectual. Yet it must embody the biblical understanding that the cognitive dimension does not exhaust either the human person, reality as a whole or the truth of God. Nor can we continue to collapse the truths of rational certainty that typify modernity. Rather, our theology must give place to the concept of 'mystery' – not as an irrational aspect alongside the rational, but as a reminder of the fundamentally non-rational or supra-rational reality of God . . . At the heart of being a Christian is a personal encounter with God in Christ which shapes and moulds us and which unites us with the community of believers. On the basis of this encounter, we seek to bring into an understandable whole the diverse strands of our personal lives and the incorporation of our lives in that faith community . . . It is in this context of making sense out of life by means of recounting the story of a transformative religious experience that theological prepositions find their importance. No experience occurs in a vacuum; no transformation comes to us apart from an interpretation facilitated by the concepts – the web of belief – we bring to it. On the contrary, experience and interpretive concepts are reciprocally related. Our concepts facilitate the experiences we have in life; at the same time, our experiences determines the interpretive concepts we employ to speak about our lives.[34]

The Rise of Spiritual Sensitivity: a Preoccupation with the Supernatural

The millennial generation will be a spiritually sensitive generation. This generation will be shaped by a spiritual renaissance where moderation, self-discipline and spiritual growth – not the accumulation of material wealth – will become the goals of the individual.[35] Celente believes that this generation will embrace people with strong spiritual or moral messages as their heroes. These heroes will be people who can be believed, as evidenced in their desire to do things for the betterment of all living creatures and not for their own personal agendas.[36]

F. Warner notes that the 1990s, preceding the next millennium, is a time when the search for spiritual guidance is on the rise.[37] Organized religion will not serve as the solution to the developing spiritual thirst that the millennial generation will acquire. Statistics support this rise in spirituality. Gallup polls for December 1994 show that 90 per cent of those surveyed believe in heaven, as opposed to 85 per cent in 1968, and that 60 per cent claim that religion is very important to their own lives. Baby boomers and generation Xers paved the way for the millennial generation by making a return to Church the fashionable thing.[38] This projects an acceptance of religion as a viable solution to life issues. Yet there remains a hollowness that the millennial generation will fill with spirituality or mysticism. The media has also aided in the creation of the spiritual thirst that the millennial generation has acquired.

From childhood this generation has been raised on cable television programmes that focused on the supernatural: the *Care Bears*, *Power Rangers*, *Teenage Mutant Ninja Turtles*, *Gnomes*, to name a few. These became the entertainment for the first-wave millennials. In more recent years, television shows like *Touched by an Angel*, *The X Files*, *Millennium*, *Sabrina the Teenage Witch*, *Nickelodeon's The Secret World of Alex Mac*, and movies like *Phenomenon*, *The Prophecy*, *Frighteners*, *Immortal Kombat*, *The Craft*, *Powder*, *The Preacher's Wife*, *Michael* and *Matilda* all dealt with supernatural, paranormal, spiritual or occultic themes, and this list is not exhaustive. Television documentaries on angels and miracles, books about supernatural occurrences and speculative theories on extraterrestrial life are a steady diet on which the millennial generation has been weaned.

Laqueur makes a strong connection between post-modern thought and the rise in spirituality. He proposes that this truth-in-everythingism leads the post-modernist to embrace new creeds, cults, fundamentalism, Christianity, Islam, Judaism, New Age religions, the occult, astrology and so on.[39] All of this points to the fact that the adolescent of the twenty-first century will be extremely spiritually sensitive. That adolescent will seek a connectedness to something supernatural that will empower, transform and fulfil their existence. Youth ministry stands in the gap of an incredible opportunity for the power of God to be demonstrated. Youth ministers will play a strategic role in the life of the adolescent, as friend, family member, hero, mentor and spiritual guide; as they have always done in past generations, but this time with a keener perspective.

CHAPTER 4

Goodness, Gracious, Great Balls of Fire! Can Youth Ministry Help Foster Morality in Young People?

SAM RICHARDS

Introduction

The late 1990s, like many transition periods in history, is marked by an increasing concern about morality in general, and the morality of the young in particular. Moral panics and crusades make regular headlines. In February 1997, the SCAA (the School Curriculum and Assessment Authority) reported their recommendations to the government regarding morality and education. While the world of secular education addresses the issue 'can we teach children to be good?',[1] it would seem timely for the Christian community to ask 'can youth ministry help foster morality in young people?'

When this apparently straightforward question is examined in its constituent parts, it becomes clear that addressing it fully is a huge task, certainly one that is beyond the scope of this paper. We need to consider what we mean by 'morality', how it might be fostered in a morally consistent way, what the particular needs and concerns of young people are in this area, and what youth ministry might be able to offer the young people and the Christian community it seeks to serve. In order to cover the necessary ground, we shall have to keep to the path rather than admire the scenery or explore every possibility.

Morality

Attempting to arrive at a definition of morality that adequately includes all the facets of this multidimensional aspect of human life, while making sufficient distinction between morality and other areas, has kept moral philosophers occupied for centuries. Let us use 'operating as a moral agent within the moral area'[2] as a working definition in the 'logical geography' of morality, for we cannot begin without a starting point.

Experts in the field of moral education have suggested that 'morality is neither good motives nor right reason nor resolute action; it is all three.'[3] An exploration of the separate processes of caring, judging and acting may help us to map out something of the form and content of morality.

Morality

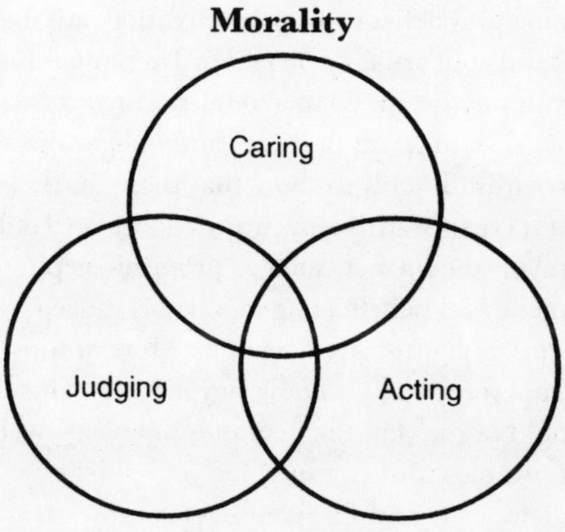

Caring

There is an affective dimension to morality. Emotivism demonstrates the problems of taking this to a subjective extreme. A. J. Ayer argues moral judgements are not descriptive statements of fact, but, rather, they convey and influence emotional attitudes.[4] Making a moral judgement in this case expresses one's feelings in the form of approval or disapproval, and tries to persuade others to share those feelings. Yet, however, much non-moral discourse uses language to convey and influence emotional attitudes (for example, advertising); and conflict is possible between our moral judgements and our emotional responses, so the latter cannot be a necessary characteristic of the former. Indeed, emotivism assumes that it is our emotions (such as horror or disgust) that cause us to make the moral judgement (expressing our disapproval), whereas we only experience emotional feelings as a result of our already holding certain beliefs (that is, it is because we judge the action to be morally wrong that we feel horror and revulsion).[5]

Christians would want to refute the common implicit form of emotivism that claims morality is just a matter of personal belief, and that if it feels right for you, then it *is* right. None the less, they would agree that morality is not a purely intellectual exercise and that motivation is an important feature.

Three main approaches to moral motivation have been espoused: duty, virtue and concern for others. For Immanuel Kant, morality flows not from any desire for personal reward or satisfaction, but from what we owe in terms of duties and obligations to others and ourselves. Yet it is difficult to show that these duties or obligations do not in fact serve the self in some way or another (if only by upholding some universal contract, such as promise-keeping, from which the moral agent also benefits in general) or, indeed, that there are genuine moral obligations to oneself. More importantly, much morality is supererogatory – going beyond mere duty.[6] Christians, likewise, would argue that the demands of love go well beyond the demands of ordinary duty (if sued for your shirt give 'your coat as well', Matthew 5.40, and forgive 'seventy times seven', Matthew 18.22), and love is not to be made into a duty or obligation, but to be freely given, as freely it is received.[7]

For Aristotle, motivation in morality is about aspiration rather than obligation. Morality is seen as the pursuit of virtue. The virtuous person is held up as someone we would want to be, and the wicked or self-indulgent person is an object of pity and scorn. 'Moral virtue is crucially a question of self-respect and self-improvement, a matter of significant personal achievement'.[8]

Christians would agree with such a teleological (purposeful) concept of human life, hold Jesus up as the model of virtue and aspire to becoming imitators of Christ – without seeing this as a selfish goal or one they were capable of achieving through human effort alone, but only in cooperation with the Holy Spirit.

Aristotle suggests that feelings or passions are crucial in morality. D. Carr identifies two different kinds of virtue in terms of the role of feeling.[9] First, virtues of self-control over feeling, such as courage, which involves control of fear, but without fear might not be courage at all. Second, virtues of attachment, such as generosity, which involve feelings of care and concern for others.

This brings us to the third area of motivation – concern for others. 'Morality is about human beings, their needs and how these needs are to be met.' Christians can agree with this for it does 'not deny that man is the creation of God – any more than to say that physics is about the natural world is to deny that the natural world is the creation of God'.[10] Morality, therefore, concerns human life and human flourishing.

Concern for others will then result from a 'view of man', fundamental beliefs and assumptions about the nature of human beings and what constitutes human flourishing. Christianity views humanity as fallen but redeemable. Here Christian belief directly affects the content of morality. Human flourishing can only fully be understood in terms of the 'inescapable relation in which man stands to God, whether man recognizes it or not'.[11] This has personal and interpersonal dimensions – what is good for individuals, for society and for humanity in general. The well-being of man is grounded in the goodwill of God and the establishing of His good Kingdom. Our ability to care is therefore related to our understanding of people's needs: feeling thus involves knowledge.

Judging

There is an evaluative dimension to morality. Morality does not bypass reason, but engages it in the process of making decisions.

R. S. Peters views morality as essentially rational. When someone asks 'What ought I to do?', there are alternatives open to him and he is asking for reasons for adopting one alternative rather than another.[12] Peters maintains that he is thereby accepting the importance of seeking reasons for action, and is also acknowledging implicitly the validity of certain moral principles by asking the question in the first place. This is a rather circular argument – only when one is playing the moral game (asking the moral question), can one appreciate and perhaps make explicit the moral rules.[13] This does, however, allow that it is reasonable for Christians to ground the moral claim in God's good and gracious will and, when uncertain what to do, to enquire after the will of God.

In potential conflict to this, a key quality of moral judgement is generally regarded to be independence of judgement as opposed to merely obeying some authority. We are not acting as moral agents if we just do what we are told. Jean-Paul Sartre takes this to the extreme position of disallowing any reference to outside authority. A. S. Neill, in turn, pursues this to its logical educational conclusion, that 'the external imposition on children of adult conceptions and values is a great sin against childhood . . . The child should not do anything until he comes to the opinion – his own opinion – that it should be done'.[14] Yet this statement itself claims authority and gives a moral judgement! Surely this demonstrates the impossibility of inventing morality for oneself in a vacuum, and the necessity of moral judgement in evaluating the available moral authorities. As John Wilson argues, we have to 'abandon both the blind faith in institutionalized authority and the equally blind rejection of any authority at all, even the authority of rational procedures.[15]

> We do in practice value the moral advice and guidance of some people more highly than others, not just 'because they say it's right', but because they may have previously directed our attention to the moral aspects of situations in a way which we have found illuminating . . . we are ourselves making a moral appraisal of their qualifications.[16]

Thus, the Bible or Jesus may be accepted as morally authoritative if we, as moral agents, have good reasons for paying heed to them. Moreover, God does not seek to elicit 'unquestioning obedience, but a willing and wholehearted love'.[17] He wants sons not slaves; it is His grace that suggests an ethic of response rather than obedience.

Likewise, we do well to regard moral conscience as rational (as opposed to the irrational guilt or fear resulting from an internalized Freudian superego sometimes ambiguously referred to as 'conscience'). A. Kolnai provides a useful definition of 'conscience in the established and dignified sense of moral self-criticism, judgement and belief – which . . . expresses the agent's endeavour to ponder and argue his decisions in universally valid terms and to make his conduct justifiable in the open court of objective morality'.[18] For Christians, this seat of moral reasoning is God-given. 'The Lord gave us mind and conscience; we cannot hide from ourselves' (Proverbs 20.27).

Kolnai raises the final aspect of judgement we shall consider – that of being universally valid. Logical impartiality or universalizability simply mean that if a moral consideration holds good for anyone, it holds good for everyone in a similar situation.

This rational principle for moral reasoning does not imply particular content – the pursuit of one's own interests is logically as good an example as loving one's neighbour as oneself (although not necessarily as practical).[19] This principle again emphasizes the role of judgement in morality – judging whether a moral reason is universally valid in the first place, then discerning if the particular circumstance is, indeed, a similar situation. Given 'do not commit murder' as a universal principle, judgement still needs to be exercised as to whether abortion, contraception, euthanasia, death in war or capital punishment are indeed murder.

Acting

There is a practical dimension to morality. While actions have no moral status outside of a person's motivations or judgements, if moral caring and reasoning never find expression in behaviour, we may have serious grounds to doubt the morality of these internal processes.[20] This dimension, with one or two notable exceptions, seems to have received much less attention from philosophers than have the others.

Utilitarianism is an 'ends' rather than 'means' approach to morality. To be moral is 'so to act as to ensure that the greatest number of people enjoy the greatest amount of happiness'.[21]

Clearly there are problems with this, for we can never possibly know all the effects of our actions and, therefore, according to this view, we can never know whether what we decide to do is morally right or wrong. Moreover, this reduces the significance of the moral agent to that of being the cause of certain consequences. Human morality becomes merely a 'machinery for getting a particular job done. It has value only in so far as it serves a purpose. If there were any other machinery which could do the job more efficiently, then this should be substituted for morality'.[22] Christianity counters this by emphasizing the freedom God has given His creation and the commission He gives to humanity to be his co-workers.

Prescriptivism also emphasizes action. R. M. Hare argues that morality is a language the function of which is to guide conduct – to give prescriptive answers about what to do.[23] Clearly the translation of moral reasoning into action is an important aspect of morality. Prescriptivism is unhelpful, though, in seeking to make this a sufficient definition of morality, for this effectively excludes judgements that are not acted on, and thereby denies the possibility of moral weakness. Yet, as Neil Cooper argues, 'between principles and practice, ideal and fulfilment, there will in any normal morality be a gap – this gappiness is an essential feature of the moral life and is made manifest in the tension which may exist prior to action between principle and desire'.[24] Christians are familiar with this gap between conscience and will, between desire and action: 'For what I do is not the good I want to do; no, the evil I do not want to do – this I keep on doing' (Romans 7.19). This is the doctrine of sin in action, and Paul continues, 'What a wretched man I am! Who will rescue me from this body of death? Thanks be to God – through Jesus Christ our Lord!' (Romans 7.24–25, NIV).

Fostering Morality in Young People

Having highlighted some of the major facets of morality, and shown that Christian morality is not logically inconsistent with either philosophical reasoning nor the total context in which Christians see human life, we can now turn our attention to the question of how morality might be fostered among young people.

We shall keep the framework of examining caring, judging and acting in turn, while reminding ourselves that morality is located in the intersection of these three dimensions, rather than in any one in isolation. Neither can we compel anyone to feel a right motivation, to accept good reason nor to act in a particular way and claim to be fostering morality – rather we would be engaged in brainwashing, propaganda and conditioning. There can be no direct or certain method for fostering morality, there are no guaranteed approaches that do not remove human freedom and thereby deny the opportunity of 'operating as a moral agent within the moral area'.[25]

Fostering Caring

When morality is seen as the pursuit of virtue, motivated by aspiration rather than obligation, then a model of virtue is helpful to foster this aspiration. Clearly Christ is the ultimate Christian model, but an incarnational approach to youth ministry would also give the youth worker a position of role model. A good role model 'is not the one, however, who is constantly extolling these virtues, so much as the one through whose conduct these virtues shine forth as examples to those in his charge and who is constantly concerned to encourage these qualities in others'.[26] Being cared for encourages the response of care, and builds the inclination of care for others. Thus the climate of youth ministry needs to be one of caring if it is to foster this attitude in young people.

Our motivation to care will also be grounded in our fundamental beliefs. The Christian 'belief in a caring God provides an unusually coherent logical context for us as carers . . . Selfless care is an expression of how we believe things are at their most profound level'.[27] In particular, our view of humanity will affect our feelings towards others. Christianity makes particular claims that all people are children of God, made in His image, loved by Him and, as our neighbour, deserving of our love. J. P. White argues that, as moral agents, we cannot avoid basing our decisions about how to behave towards others partly on our most fundamental beliefs and assumptions,[28] so young people need to be clear about their view of humanity. Youth ministry should provoke young people to articulate and explore the adequacy of the beliefs they actually hold as well as to consider the implications of the Christian faith in this area.

Shaver (in the rationale-building model of moral education[29]) discusses the importance of nurturing the motive to care by giving opportunities to practise caring behaviours. Youth ministry should be able to provide a wealth of such opportunities, from young people working together in small or large groups towards common goals, to acts of service for people in the wider community. This should provide a context in which the value of caring is experienced positively (as opposed to punitively in 'community service orders'!) while the rational justification for such behaviour can be explored. At the same time, knowledge of the different perspectives of others helps to develop empathy, a key ingredient in caring.

Fostering Judging

L. Kohlberg (in the cognitive development theory of moralization[30]) argues that social perspective-taking is crucial to moral development. Expanding the work of Jean Piaget in the area of moral reasoning, he describes three broad levels in development:

> The first level most often characterizes children's moral reasoning; still, many adolescents and some adults persist in this reasoning. The second level usually arises during preadolescence, comes into fuller prominence during adolescence, and remains dominant in the thinking of most adults. The third level is rarest. It arises, if at all, during adolescence or early adulthood and characterizes the reasoning of only a minority of adults.[31]

Clearly, according to this view, adolescence is a key period in moral development.

In terms of caring, Kohlberg sheds light on both the social perspective taken and the motivation this provides at each level (see table at the end of this chapter). These develop as follows. In level one, from the egocentric pursuit of own interests and avoidance of punishment to an awareness that everyone has interests to pursue and attainment of fairness or equality for self. In level two, from taking the perspective of other individuals in relationships and being seen as a good person by significant others as well as self to taking a societal point of view and upholding the system. In level three, taking a prior-to-society perspective and upholding universal moral principles. While Christians (and many others) would take issue with Kohlberg's appraisal of moral development being purely in terms of cognitive reasoning rather than 'what he rather derisively terms the "bag of virtues" approach'[32] and also the 'male bias' of both his sample and structure of moral reasoning (see C. Gilligan[33] and others), they should not thereby dismiss his important claims, which have direct application to the task of fostering morality in young people.

Kohlberg gives a pattern for the development of perspective-taking ability linked to cognitive ability that the Church does well to heed. While a child may appropriately base morality on a (fairly physical) fear of displeasing God and being punished, an adolescent should have developed the ability to place oneself in another's shoes and thereby have some understanding of how to care as a good Samaritan. Likewise, appreciation of the commandments should have developed from believing them to be kept or else to an understanding of how the community benefits from operating within them. Kohlberg also argues that it is possible to move beyond this level of reasoning, beyond seeking the fulfilment of the law, to seeking the spirit of the law or the fundamental principles that underlie it: 'Love the Lord your God with all your heart, with all your soul, with all your strength, and with all your mind and love your neighbour as you love yourself' (Luke 10.27, GNB).

If youth ministry is to foster morality, then it must facilitate and encourage development in moral reasoning. Kohlberg's work has shown that:

> what motivates students toward greater cognitive sophistication is exposure to more adequate patterns of reasoning, specifically those that reflect a stage of moral judgement one higher than their own. When individuals are forced to consider approaches to moral conflicts that are more comprehensive and consistent than those they are used to, cognitive 'disequilibrium' results. The power of a more adequate logic is unsettling yet enticing. Over time, the encounter with higher-level thinking stimulates the self-development of a more advanced stage.[34]

Christianity has nothing to fear from the 'more advanced stage' of moral reasoning. Yet, all too often, the Church is content to present moral rhetoric consistent with earlier stages rather than risk the unsettling process of 'disequilibrium'. This leaves young people particularly vulnerable as they will undoubtedly encounter moral reasoning at more advanced levels in other arenas (such as school, the media, politics and so on), which will be presenting alternative values and beliefs with enticing logic. These young people deserve to have encountered Christian morality expressed to the same level of cognitive reasoning so that they genuinely can choose between the ethics rather than the reasoning. If youth ministry is not to fail young people in this area, it needs to grapple with the work of Kohlberg and explore strategies for presenting and stimulating Christian moral reasoning at all levels. How many young people presently drift from the Church precisely because they encounter moral dilemmas (such as whether or not to have pre-marital sex or use illegal drugs as opposed to legal ones) for which they find the offered Christian rhetoric insubstantial and juvenile?

Indeed, Jesus' approach to moral education could be viewed as precisely this task of exposing moral agents (the Pharisees, the rich young man, Martha and so on) to another perspective, challenging their reasoning as well as their conclusions, and enticing them to a more adequate morality. 'Moral judgements are typically characterized by their generality, universality, logical consistency, objectivity, detachment and impartiality'.[35] Many of these skills can be stimulated by discussion of hypothetical and real moral issues within a genuinely open atmosphere, where young people are free from both peer pressure and the pressure to please authority, free to voice opinions, take on roles, question. Indeed, encouraging such discussion can also develop the skill of judging an issue to be within the moral area in the first place.

Fostering Acting

F. Newmann (in the social action model of moral education[36]) argues that young people may not even address the question 'what should I do?' if they are powerless to affect moral outcomes. If there are no real alternatives, why should they engage in moral deliberation? 'Students must feel a measure of control over their environment in order for effective moral thinking to take place'.[37]

Youth ministry, if it is to foster moral action, needs to enable young people to have an impact, within the youthwork itself, within the faith community and within the wider community. This means so structuring the youthwork and the Church that young people are participants at every level of policy and practice. It means allowing both the youthwork and the Church to be open and responsive to the scrutiny of young people. It means engaging in moral discussion about the immediate context and relationships as and when moral issues arise. It also means that the Church needs to be engaging in larger social and political issues, to demonstrate that Christian morality does not stop at the boundary of the faith community, but extends into public life in our pluralistic and secular society.

Virtue is not to be found exclusively in the private domain or the public domain – there is 'an intrinsic connection between personal character and public morality',[38] and therefore morality needs to find expression in both domains. The Church needs to practise what it preaches, and allow young people the opportunity to do the same. Indeed, young people tend to be both especially critical of hypocrisy and idealistic in their vision, seeing no daylight between conviction and action in the public realm. Youth ministry needs to enable young people to flex their moral muscles in direct action.

Conclusions

The SCAA is about to recommend that State education respond to the present demand for morality in the following three ways. First, by addressing the moral issues intrinsic to existing subjects. Second, by adding morality and citizenship to the curriculum. Third, by schools modelling a 'moral community' by means of their ethos.[39] Youth ministry has good grounds to claim the ability to make a distinctive contribution in each of these areas.

First, morality is, or should be, addressed as an important intrinsic aspect of everything in either programmes or relationships in youth ministry. Second, it is, or should be, an explicit part of any formal or informal curriculum in youth ministry. Third, the Church, and therefore youth ministry, has the ability to be a moral community based on commitment to a shared story, a narrative of faith from which values are derived.

The Church can also provide empirical evidence for its ability to foster morality. The European Value Systems Study Group's surveys in 1981 and 1990 consistently show that those who regularly go to church have more distinctive positions both on standard items of Christian belief and on a variety of moral concerns than those who don't go to church. It also shows that those involved in unpaid voluntary work are typically more religious in belief and practice than those who are uninvolved.[40] This is confirmed by the research among young people by Kay and Francis, which demonstrates a link between belonging to a church and a more positive attitude towards others, themselves and traditional Christian moral values.[41]

This may begin to answer A. MacIntyre's plea for

> the construction of local forms of community within which civility and the intellectual and moral life can be sustained through the new dark ages which are already upon us. And if the tradition of the virtues was able to survive the horrors of the last Dark Ages, we are not entirely without grounds for hope. This time, however, the barbarians are not waiting beyond the frontiers; they have already been governing us for quite some time. And it is our lack of consciousness of this that constitutes part of our predicament.[42]

S. Hauerwas and W. Willimon argue that young people need religious roots, not the wings of liberalism. We cannot liberate youth by telling them to 'think for themselves' – this simply abandons them to think with the aid of dominant cultural images supplied by consumer capitalism. Rather, we must initiate them into the community of 'resident aliens' that confesses and practises the Christian Story.[43] 'Christian practices are things Christians do together over time in response to and in the light of God's active presence for the life of the world.[44] As a result of participation in these practices, our moral imagination and our daily activity are shaped in powerful and fundamental ways. When the Church teaches these practices well, parents outside the faith community send their children precisely because they see the Church fostering morality. When the Church does not do this well, those parents look for other activities (such as sport or performing arts) that they see as character-forming.[45]

Faith communities are not the only moral communities in society (for example gangs, the Green movement and so on). Nor do all churches or youth ministries live up to the ideals of *agape* and *koinonia*. Yet they are unique in their central activity of worship. In worship:

> individuals who believe in theory that there is a God who cares, and who encourages them to care, are now confronted with this God . . . We open our hearts and minds to the presence of God and ask God, in turn, to shape our hearts and minds . . . All the worshipper can say is that within worship moral values take on a more demanding and insistent shape than they do outside worship . . . It requires no less than we should go out into the world to love, to serve and to care.[46]

It is possible for youth ministry to help foster morality among young people. The question now is whether or not it will.

Kohlberg's Six Stages of Moral Judgement

	Content of Stage		
Level and Stage	**What is Right**	**Reasons for Doing Right**	**Social Perspective of Stage**
Level 1: Pre-conventional Stage 1: Heteronomous morality	Sticking to rules backed by punishment; obedience for its own sake; avoiding physical damage to persons and property	Avoidance of punishment, superior power of authorities.	*Egocentric point of view.* Doesn't consider the interests of others or recognize that they differ from the actor's; doesn't relate two points of view. Actions considered physically rather than in terms of psychological interests of others. Confusion of authority's perspective with one's own.

continued overleaf

	Content of Stage		
Level and Stage	**What is Right**	**Reasons for Doing Right**	**Social Perspective of Stage**
Stage 2: Individualism, instrumental purpose and exchange	Following rules only when in one's immediate interest; acting to meet one's own interests and needs and letting others do the same. Right is also what is fair or what is an equal exchange, deal, agreement.	To serve one's own needs or interests in a world where one has to recognize that other people also have interests.	*Concrete individualistic perspective.* Aware that everybody has interests to pursue and that these can conflict; right is relative (in the concrete individualistic sense).
Level II: Conventional Stage 3: Mutual interpersonal expectations, relationships and interpersonal conformity	Living up to what is expected by people close to you or what people generally expect of a good son, brother, friend, etc. 'Being good' is important and means having good motives, showing concern for others. It also means keeping mutual relationships such as trust, loyalty, respect and gratitude.	The need to be a good person in your own eyes and those of others; caring for others; belief in the Golden Rule; desire to maintain rules and authority that support stereotypical good behaviour.	*Perspective of the individual in relationships with other individuals.* Aware of shared feelings, agreements and expectations that take primacy over individual interests. Relates points of view through the concrete Golden Rule, putting oneself in the other guy's shoes. Does not yet consider generalized system perspective.
Level II: Conventional (continued) Stage 4: Social system and conscience	Fulfilling duties to which you have agreed; laws to be upheld except in extreme cases where they conflict with other fixed social duties. Right is also contributing to the society, group or institution.	To keep the institution going as a whole and avoid a breakdown in the system 'if everyone did it'; imperative of conscience to meet one's defined obligations. (Easily confused with Stage 3 belief in rules and authority.)	*Differentiates societal point of view from interpersonal agreement or motives.* Takes the point of view of the system that defines roles and rules; considers individual relations in terms of place in the system.

continued

Level and Stage	What is Right	Reasons for Doing Right	Social Perspective of Stage
	Content of Stage		
Level III: Post-conventional or Principled Stage 5: Social contract or utility and individual rights	Being aware that people hold a variety of values and opinions and that most of their values and rules are relative to their group. Relative rules usually upheld in the interest of impartiality and because they are the social contract. Some non-relative values and rights (such as 'life' and 'liberty') must be upheld in any society and regardless of majority opinion.	A sense of obligation to law because of one's social contract to make and abide by laws for the welfare of all and for the protection of all people's rights. A feeling of contractual commitment, freely entered into, to family, friendship, trust and work obligations. Concern that laws and duties be based on rational calculation of overall utility, 'the greatest good for the greatest number.'	*Prior-to-society perspective.* Rational individual aware of values and rights prior to social attachments and contracts. Integrates perspectives by formal mechanisms of agreement, contract, objective impartiality and due process. Considers moral and legal points of view; recognizes that they sometimes conflict and finds it difficult to integrate them.
Level III: Post-conventional or Principled (continued) Stage 6: Universal ethical principles	Following self-chosen ethical principles. Particular laws or social agreements usually valid because they rest on such principles; when laws violate these principles, one acts in accordance with principle. Principles are universal principles of justice: equality of human rights and respect for the dignity of human beings as individuals.	The belief as a rational person in the validity of universal moral principles and a sense of personal commitment to them.	*Perspective of a moral point of view from which social arrangements derive.* Perspective is that of a rational individual recognizing the nature of morality or the fact that persons are ends in themselves and must be treated as such.

Source: 'The Six Stages of Moral Judgement', table from *Moral Stages and Moralization: The Cognitive-Developmental Approach* by Lawrence Kohlberg. In *Moral Development and Behaviour: Theory, Research and Social Issues*, edited by Thomas Lickona, 1976, Holt, Rinehart and Winston.

CHAPTER 5

Ethical Heroism, Christian Empathy and Youth Empowerment: Biblical and Philosophical Initiatives to Empower the Young via Evangelistic Social Action

REVEREND NELSON ELWOOD COPELAND, JR

Introduction: The Goal – Creating Leaders

There is a clear biblical directive to empower the young towards empathetic leadership that is grounded in spiritual excellence and public heroism. The young people of this planet are a valuable resource. They are dichotomous beings as they are the presence of the future. Henry Thoreau rightly said, 'Every child begins the world again',[1] as they are a minor portion of today's reality, but a major segment of all our tomorrows. They seek a brighter day, but many adults and nations have failed them. They want hope, but some find only empty promises. The time has come for a heroic new agenda of youth empowerment to rise from the soils of every international city and town, an agenda involving courageous youth leadership. The *zeitgeist*[2] (spirit of the times, acceptable cultural climate) is now.

The future of any youth programme that is to make a genuine difference is recognized by its investment in creating leaders. Yes, we need to create them! Rarely are leaders born – they are made by means of an investment on the youth workers' part to mentor, disciple, and involve adolescents in social justice issues. No adolescent should be so undervalued as to assume that they lack positive leadership ability.

First of all, leadership begins with vision. Youth outreach or ministry must work to open the eyes of every blinded Saul and help them become a Paul. Teenagers want a better future and will often wait for a mentor to provide them with a dream to pursue. Refuse this offer. Instead, provide them with the dignity needed to create their own dreams and aspirations. They must then lead themselves in order for the vision to become reality. This is the essence of empowerment.

Second, leadership continues with introspective power, which is nothing more and nothing less than creative self-discipline. It is the power to lead others by leading oneself. A good external leader must simultaneously become an internal leader, because introspective power is a holistic process that is increased by choosing to organize oneself from within. Simply put, self-discipline is the power to lead.

Third, leadership is directed towards reproduction. Genuine leadership is rarely satisfied by the act of leading. Pleasure is found in raising up others, because no leader will last forever. Any youth programme or community that has hope for tomorrow is reproducing its leaders today, in an act of love rooted in the heroic desire to see teens maximize their potential.

Let us set about the business of creating leaders who desire social, economic and spiritual transformation. The problems facing our profession are far from impossible to conquer, as long as adults and youth are willing to work, pray and struggle together to create for themselves a new agenda that will focus on the objectives of Christ. Let us apply ourselves with the same vigour as does the Salvation Army song, which provides an image of the impact Christian leadership can have.[3]

> The Army is coming – amen, amen!
> To conquer this city for Jesus – amen!
> We'll shout 'Hallelujah' and praise His dear name,
> Who redeemed us to God through the blood of the Lamb.
> The sound of His footsteps is rolling along;
> The kingdom of Satan, triumphant so long,
> Is shaking and tott'ring and downward shall fall
> For Jesus, the Saviour, shall reign over all.

The sound of salvation shall float on the wind –
Through street, court and alley its way shall it find,
The stubborn to break, and the broken to bind,
For Jesus is mighty, yet gentle and kind.[4]

The Task: Youth Empowerment

The goal should not simply be to empower adolescents spiritually, but also socially within the youth programme setting. Within the next 20 years, our profession will be challenged to stretch our parochial concepts of youth ministry to become much more global in scope and practice. With the existence of faster mail services, the Internet and the Worldwide Web, we can connect privileged adolescents across continents and work towards similar goals, create prayer partners, Bible studies and meetings across oceans. Today youth ministry has the opportunity to share in the joys and pains of one another no matter if one lives in Harlem, USA, or Seoul in Korea, Owerri in Nigeria, or Lima in Peru. However, this is not economically and technologically possible in all our contexts.

No longer can those of us who are beneficiaries of Western civilization continue to promote only Western concepts of youth outreach lest we take the risk of closing out the majority of the Christian world. A worldwide shift in the centre of gravity of Christianity is occurring, so that the heartlands of the Church are no longer in Europe exclusively and decreasingly in North America, but are found in Latin America, in certain parts of Asia and Africa. For example, 'while every day in the West, roughly 7,500 people in effect stop being Christians, every day in Africa roughly double that number become Christians.' The expansion of Christianity in Africa in the twentieth century has often been referred to as 'the fourth great age of Christian expansion'. Using conservative statistics, in 1900 there were 10 million African Christians, in 1970, 143 million and by the year 2000 there will be roughly 393 million African Christians. That means that one in five Christians worldwide will be Black African.[5] Western youth ministry has yet to corporately take a serious look at the African continent, which is ripe for youthwork as it is reported that 60–75 per cent of the entire continent is under the age of 25. Yes, it is a continent of young people.

In a similar vein, a number of adolescents feel they have no power over their own destiny. Worldwide, our youth need opportunities for ownership in their neighbourhoods and youth groups, which may translate into sending teams of adolescents to community meetings so they can know and respond to the decisions being made over them, or giving more leadership to youth in the youth group. After all, the best youth leaders lead least because they empower their members to lead. Empowerment is crucial to harmony in youth culture. Wherever there has been unrest in youth culture, it has come on the coat tails of a group of young people realizing they have not the power over their own destiny that is due them. Those of us entrusted to do youth ministry must share whatever power we have with them if true youth empowerment is to take place. It is a disservice and a lie to tell teenagers to come to a 'youth group' that, in reality, is not guided by them at all. It would be better to call it a 'youth pastor group'.

Young people will obtain the power due them one way or another, whether negatively (say by joining a gang, being profitable in the drug market, acting disorderly in the youth group or taking part in a riot) or positively (for example, excelling in sports, music, drama, academic life and youth group leadership). Urban youth deserve the opportunity to utilize their God-given skills and control some of the institutions that affect their lives. The youth group is one conduit through which urban youth empowerment can be expressed. It is dangerous to disempower youth, because it makes celibate their aspirations, bankrupt their hopes and defers their dreams.[6]

Interlude: Youth Empowerment is Ministry Double Dutch-style

In the United States, there is a game called 'double dutch', which is popular among African-American teenagers. This game in some way poetically parallels a typical lower-economic teenager's life. It is similar to the activity jump-rope where one person jumps over a single turning rope until they tire, except, in double dutch, there are two ropes turned simultaneously by two people, one clockwise, the other criss-crossing counter-clockwise. The objective is to see who can remain in the centre the longest without getting the ropes entangled around their feet.

Daring anyone to jump in and begin the game, the rope turners start by saying 'Challenge! Challenge!'. When a challenger feels confident, they lunge into the ropes while they are turning. If the jumper successfully makes it in, everyone begins to count aloud 'One, two, three, four, five . . .' as the person hops, continuing to count until the jumper either tires or miscalculates the ropes and gets entangled. Whoever remains within the ropes longest is the winner.

This is the story of the myriad of adolescents we serve who feel they must navigate the difficult 'ropes' of life every day. They must overcome every obstacle that comes their way, with little time to think. They never have a chance to respond proactively, only reactively. As the ropes outlast any individual, even the strongest fall and the finest stumble, leaving a wasteland of the former dreams and hopes of any person who can survive long enough for a chance at life.

The weak fade away into apathetic despair, wondering if anyone could ever survive; the strong try again, like Albert Camus' Sisyphus, forever pushing a heavy rock up a slope despite knowing it will roll back again each time it reaches the peak. 'He knows that he shall never win his hill, yet he refuses to allow his rock to remain at the bottom of the slope.' His persistence allowed Sisyphus to keep a 'hold on his human dignity in the face of an absurd world', yet even he understood the futility of his efforts.[7]

Many of the young people we serve are searching for someone who can help them survive the ropes of poor education, joblessness, inadequate health care, single parent homes, political and economic disenfranchisement, violence, sexual diseases and gangs. They are searching, yet no one has withstood the test. The apparent permanence of these 'double dutch' ropes in real life will cause even the most determined young person or youth worker to become discouraged and cry out as did the prophet Habakkuk (Habakkuk 1.2–4):

How long, O Lord, must I call for help,
but you do not listen?
Or cry out to you 'Violence!'
but you do not save?
Why do you make me look at injustice?
Why do you tolerate wrong?
Destruction and violence are before me;
there is strife, and conflict abounds.
Therefore the law is paralysed,
and justice never prevails.
The wicked hem in the righteous,
so that justice is perverted.

Many have come to these teens with good ideas, philosophies and approaches for success, which over time have failed or their relevance has expired. Others have given training seminars and positive thinking classes that allow young people to survive for longer periods of time. Not many of us, however, have asked or answered the more fundamental question, 'who is able to cut the ropes?' Let me be bold by stating that teenagers do not want the ropes at all. Ropes entangle their potential. Teaching them how to avoid them is not enough – they will eventually get caught and tire. Instead, youth need to realize that Jesus is the only double dutch champion. He will not only jump with them as they face daily trials, he will cut the ropes for those who trust in him.[8] Matthew 19.26 is clear – with women and men this is impossible, but 'with God all things are possible'.

Our single most important hope is that by ministering to the actual needs of young people within our own local contexts, and via interactions with multiple youth programmes, we can convince the world population of adolescents that Jesus is the most viable answer to all of their questions. What the average adolescent desires out of their spiritual life is the simple knowledge that God is not distant to their needs but is personal. All youth empowerment programmes can be valued by their ability to meet the direct personal needs of their constituents.

To give a somewhat related example, by the time the Cakchiquel Indians were being evangelized in Latin America, they already had a detailed and unique cultural ethos and language. They were taught the scriptures not by imposing the Latin Vulgate version of the Bible upon them, but by translating it into their vernacular so that everyone could read the scriptural text themselves. Later, one of the Cakchiquels, having read over the biblical text for the first time, said with great delight, 'This is wonderful! God speaks our language!'[9] In a similar fashion, good, empowering youth programmes should be presented in a living vernacular and in a form your own youth can decode.

Evangelistic Social Action: Ethical Heroism, Christian Empathy and Youth Empowerment

This paper's primary title is 'Ethical Heroism, Christian Empathy and Youth Empowerment'. It would serve my purpose to explain that these are not three differing terms, but, rather, harmonious dimensions of evangelistic social action, which is the most practical form (the author promotes) of spiritual and social youth empowerment.

Ground Zero: Evangelistic Social Action

On occasion, I hear the complaint that youth activism breeds discontent with the status quo. If so, rejoice! If we do not allow adolescents to remedy their own social situations we will lose them to a militancy or apathy that will reap evil repercussions. To act against the age-old dehumanizing exploits of reality is to stand up for self-dignity and declare, 'I am somebody, in spite of my present circumstances!'[10] Early Church father Arnobius of Sicca, in view of the many sufferings the early Church endured, concluded that Christians 'wholly deserve the odium of being public enemies . . .'[11] If we are honest about the implications of the Gospel's message, our youth may become revolutionaries by deduction. As oppressed youth discover the deep relationship between the entrenchment of societal sin and their impoverishment in life, it will become the springboard on which activism can be launched. This is why Christian social action is revolutionary – it involves adolescents in the process of Christ's concern for their own liberation.[12] Jesus has come that they might enjoy life to the fullest (John 10.10), and bring God's will to earth as it is in heaven (Matthew 6.10).

To allow adolescents to become socially involved – by protesting against a rip-off business, rejecting police brutality, or recycling, for example – is to own stock in the nation and neighbourhood they are a part of. Youth programmes need to learn about the socio-political issues that have a bearing on their community as, in doing so, they will form the building blocks of improvement.

Youth ministry at its best has elements of holistic outreach. That is, it attempts not only to 'save' the souls of individuals via evangelism, but to improve society by means of social action. A number of Christians commonly believe that evangelism and social action are opposites. On the contrary, they actually compliment each other. Both contexts exist for the purpose of conversion and both rely on the motto: 'Repent, the Kingdom of heaven is at hand'.

Evangelism exists to call individuals to repentance for their sins and lead them towards a vibrant relationship with Jesus Christ. Social action does the same, but focuses on social structures. Unifying the two creates evangelistic social action, which is a heroic social–spiritual process that seeks to simultaneously direct individuals and the structures that oppress them towards a more godly outlook. It is as much an exercise in prayer and faith as in demonstration and protest.

Evangelistic social action takes place first and foremost within the youth group, later expanding outwards into society as that which comes out from the youth group.[13] The Christian teenager ought to care enough for those who are suffering spiritually and socially to realize, as did Jonathan Edwards, that 'We are to look upon ourselves as related to all [humanity] . . .'[14] Whoever shuts his ears to the cry of the downtrodden and hurting will one day cry out and not be answered (see Proverbs 21.13). Edwards explains further:

> It is the duty of the visible people of God to give for the supply of the needy, freely, and without grudging . . . This is a duty to which God's people are under very strict obligations. It is not

> merely a commendable thing for [us] to be kind and bountiful to the poor, but our bounden duty, as much a duty as it is to pray, or to attend public worship, or anything else whatever; and the neglect of it brings great guilt upon any person.[15]

Evangelistic social action at its best bubbles from the bottom up and spills over into social matters. When adolescents get excited about personal or structural acts of social goodness, encourage them.[16] However, it is necessary, at this juncture, to closely examine the three inseparable and overlapping dimensions that make up the youth empowerment strategy of evangelistic social action.

Dimension One: Ethical Heroism

Ethical heroism is a spiritual and moral act that pursues justice in the world as a result of one's conversion experience. Christians perform ethical acts of heroism not out of a demanding duty, but desire salvation for others because Christ first saved and loved them. Our acts of heroism, then, are rooted in Christ's heroic act on the cross – that all creation might be reconciled with him via repentance. Ethical heroism in its most pure form is recognized as heroic love.

Christian adolescents who put their faith into action (not lip-service) practise heroic love – the pivot on which Christian activism and social involvement rests. Heroic love is central to the cross because it drives the Christian youth group to do evangelistic acts of grace and love. These revolutionary acts are motivated not simply by external change, but by spiritual change.[17]

Heroic love must continually be associated with toughness, durability and confrontation, rooted in the unbending love of Christ for all and in the justice God demands is due to the oppressed. In short, heroic love does resist because God 'is not a non-resistant God'.[18] It 'is action oriented; it does not avoid conflict but seeks to confront and resolve it.'[19] Heroic love is passive when it comes to taking life, and active in saving and defending life.[20]

Teenagers must become inspired to be the revolutionary instruments of Christ's heroism as He seeks to salvage joyously those who would come to Him. This form of evangelistic social action does not seek the limelight, because it is a light unto itself.[21]

Ernst Troeltsch, in *The Social Teaching of the Christian Churches*, contends that the 'ethic of Jesus is heroic' and, as such, does not 'compromise with the claims of the life of this world'.[22] Ethical heroism (heroic love) helps make the world a better dwelling place by focusing on the quality of society's soul[23] and on its impact on the individual. Simplicity and intimacy are the basic ethical imperatives that guide a young person's quest for ethical heroism.[24]

Our task as youth ministers is to provide adolescents with the chance to become the heroes of their communities. A Christian hero always has one foot in reality (that which is social) and the other in potentiality (that which is spiritual).[25] We can most distinctly improve the character of Christian young people by providing opportunities for them to make heroic sacrifices and take risks. The playwright Oscar Wilde said 'that every little action of the common day makes or unmakes character'.[26] Character-building begins once youth recognize that these risks serve the benefit of a better tomorrow. Aristotle writes much the same thing in the *Nicomachean Ethics*: 'We become just by doing just acts, temperate by doing temperate acts, brave by doing brave acts.'[27] Let us create programmes that empower both wealthy and impoverished youth to be brave as Christ was on the Cross. The Hebrew wisdom literature encourages us to remember:

> If you pursue justice, you will attain it
> and wear it as a glorious robe.
> [Just as] birds flock with their kind;
> so truth returns to those who practise it. (Sirach 27.8–9)

Dimension Two: Christian Empathy

Empathy is a tough-minded emotive action. Given this reality, moral discipline is required in the use of empathy. Evangelistic social action is emotive in practice, because it shares in the joys and pains of others. Contrary to the beliefs of a great number of philosophers (some of whom I have already quoted in other contexts), right emotion is equally as important as right reason.[28]

Plato dismissed emotions as dangerous and irrelevant, as right reason. Ignatius advised those who sought God's will to detach their emotions, and Kant defended stoic ideals, saying 'the prudent man must at no time be in a state of emotion, not even that of sympathy with [a] best friend.'[29] The assumptions that I believe are most faulty in this world view are that:

- reason can be disengaged wholly from emotion;
- detached reason is trustworthy and unbiased;
- emotions only bias and cloud moral decision making.[30]

Christian empathy provides a sense of self, as do most emotions.[31] It connects us with the caring part of reality 'and gives vividness to the experience of being alive.'[32] Empathy as an emotion is not greater than reason – it is its partner in truth. Thereby, empathy that is informed by reason can expand the meaning of God's grace further in a young person's life. These teenagers must discipline themselves towards empathetic thinking, which involves both a conceptual and perceptual commitment.[33]

Glaucon in a discussion with Plato on virtue gives an answer to the question of how to recognize a just person. The response is strikingly pre-emptive and similar to the empathy expressed by Isaiah's suffering servant and Jesus on the Cross. Glaucon responds that a just person would be one:

> of true simplicity of character who . . . wants to be and not to seem good . . . we must strip him of everything except his justice . . . He must have the worst of reputations for wrong-doing though he had done no wrong, so we can test his justice and see if he weakens in the face of unpopularity and all that goes with it. We shall give him an undeserved and lifelong reputation for wickedness and make him stick to his chosen course until his death . . . They will say that the just man, as we have pictured him, will be scourged, tortured and imprisoned, his eyes will be put out and after enduring every humiliation he will be crucified.[34]

Some years later came Jesus Christ, who not only is an example of the just person, but is the pre-eminent model of Christian empathy who, while he was being crucified, could utter nonviolently, 'Father, forgive them for they know not what they do' (Luke 23.34).

In attempting to promote Christian empathy as a means of evangelistic social action, we must, equally, not allow our empathy to lapse into paternalism or benevolent acts motivated out of an unsubstantiated sense of guilt, but, rather, they must be entered into with reciprocity in mind. As the former African leader and Christian statesman Nyerere (who urged missionaries to devote themselves to nation-building and the struggle against poverty and disease) said in a famous speech, instructing the Maryknoll Sisters, '. . . kindness is not enough; piety is not enough; and charity is not enough . . . the Church must work with the people in the positive tasks of building a future based on social justice . . . it is important that we should stress the working with, not the working for.'[35] Youth workers must view any attempt at mission in a similar manner.

Ultimately, Christian empathy, if it is to have an impact in the lives of those young people who involve themselves in evangelistic acts of social action, must involve them bathing themselves with a determination that they are going to have the same attitude

> . . . as that of Christ Jesus, who, being in the very nature God, did not consider equality with God something to be grasped, but made himself nothing, taking the very nature of a servant, being made in human likeness. And being found in appearance as a man, he humbled himself and became obedient to death – even death on a cross! Therefore, God exalted him to the highest place and gave him the name that is above every name, that at the name of Jesus every knee should bow, in heaven and on earth and under the earth, and every tongue confess that Jesus Christ is Lord, to the glory of God the Father. (Philippians 2.5–11)

Dimension Three: Biblical Youth Empowerment

Given that the early portion of this paper has addressed the basic dimensions of youth empowerment, I will not re-address this subject entirely. However, lest I be labelled a heretic and taken to be burned at a site similar to Oxford's Martyr's Memorial, it should be understood that youth empowerment in and of itself is fruitless unless the protocols of evangelistic social action are biblically sound. Heroic social deeds are common in the Christian biblical tradition.

Furthermore, there is adequate evidence that Jesus wants us to empower the young. This is implicit in his statement to his disciples who chose to keep young people away from Jesus. Jesus empowers the young by acknowledging their value to his followers with 'suffer not the little children for they are like the Kingdom of God.' (Matthew 19.13–15). As adolescents act against injustice, remind them that, in some ways, they are a better reflection of the Kingdom than the adult population in the eyes of Christ.

Further, the ability to act heroically for Christ is not simply an activity that exclusively exists for the mature, it is also for the young. The Bible itself, properly understood, encourages the greatest commandments to be practised by all believers: '"Love the Lord your God with all your heart and with all your soul and with all your mind and with all your strength." The second is this: "Love your neighbour as yourself." There is no commandment greater than these' (Mark 12.30–31). Commandments are never meant to be pondered as conditional guidelines; they must be enacted unconditionally towards those both in and outside the Christian faith.

Once again, social activism is never a replacement for serving Christ – it is an extension of one's conversion experience. We love others because Christ first loved us (1 John 4.19). 'As we have opportunity, let us do what is good to all people, but especially to the family of believers' (Ephesians 6.10). Heroic acts of love and justice extend from one's love of God. Listen to 1 John 3.17–20a at this point.

> If anyone has material possessions and sees his brother in need but has no pity on him, how can the love of God be in him? Dear children, let us not love with words or tongue but with actions and in truth. This then is how we know that we belong to the truth, and how we set our hearts at rest in his presence whenever our hearts condemn us.

While it is no secret that Martin Luther considered the Epistle of James 'an epistle of straw' the Epistle promotes itself well along the lines of this paper's reasoning:

> Be doers of the word, and not hearers only deceiving your own selves . . . What good is it, my brothers, if a man claims to have faith but has no deeds? Can faith save him? Suppose a brother or sister is without clothes and daily food. If one of you says to him, 'Go I wish you well; keep warm and well fed', but does nothing about his physical needs, what good is it? In the same way, faith by itself, if not accompanied by action is dead. But someone will say, 'You have faith; I have deeds'. Show me your faith without deeds, and I will show you my faith by what I do. As the body without the spirit is dead, so faith without works is dead. (James 1.22 KJV; 2.14–19, 26 NIV)

To empower youth, the aforementioned Scriptures are to be acknowledged as powerful departure points for evangelistic social action. We are pilgrims in this strange land, yet are not loners – in the world, but not of it. As such, we must go beyond the comfortable confines of simply enacting the biblical text within our own church walls and youth programmes, which can create a pseudo-spiritualism in adolescents. Instead, let us become inspired by the social truths and mandates within the Bible, which at its core edifies the saints and brings sinners to personal and social repentance.[36] Walter Rauschenbusch notes that while acting socially God 'strives within our striving, kindles His flame in our intellect, sends the impact of his energy to make our will restless for righteousness, floods our subconscious mind with dreams and longings, and always urges [that] . . . God [be] . . . the source of our energies, the ground of our hopes.'[37]

Jesus is a prime example of this mindset. For Hebrews 13.12–14 exhorts us towards the realization: 'And so Jesus also suffered outside the city gate to make the people holy through his own blood. Let us, then, go to him outside the camp, bearing the disgrace he bore. For here we do not have an enduring city, but we are looking for a city that is to come.'

The Final Test: Challenge and Response

I will conclude this paper with a challenge and an ethical dilemma. The ability to empower young people heroically as instruments of evangelistic social action into the next century is in close relationship with the ability of its youth workers to follow paths of spiritual excellence in their daily lives as we meet each generation's challenges together. This means that we will need to be (as much as possible) introspective spiritually and proactive publicly; to be in harmony with the Holy Spirit in us as we act socially in the mainstream. In other words, evangelistic social action causes some dissonance in practice. But, I do believe that 'the best way to get the self ready for heaven, is to get the world ready for God.' Being in God's presence must come before any evangelistic or social action. We must 'be not so busy in the Master's service that [we] have no time to be in the Master's presence.'[38]

As a young man, Arnold Toynbee had been indelibly influenced by the Great War and the death of a generation of young British soldiers. As a result, he began to ask what is it that makes one generation (or civilization) greater than another? This question drew him into a life-long study of the elements that have shaped numerous generations along the course of human history. In his *A Study of Human History*, Toynbee's thesis entitled 'challenge and response' argued that every generation will at some point encounter single or multiple challenges that will threaten its very existence and credibility. The crucial question for him, however, is how will the leadership élite respond and are they adequate to the task that is before them?[39] I contend that this question cannot yet be answered with the existing youth ministry leadership internationally. While there are great marginal efforts that exist in some circles there are few overwhelming efforts that attempt to carve through class, economic and ethnic differences within youth ministry. While I have travelled to six countries and visited all 50 of the United States within America, to some degree, my sense is that this profession has yet to attempt the full challenge of the Gospel message. Some have been more concerned with making youth conform to the accepted folk ways and mores of their given society. However, if I may persuade you, our call to discipleship should continue to be, 'do not conform to the pattern of this world, but be transformed by the renewing of your mind' (Romans 12.2). It is without denial that adolescents must operate in their given societies, but there can be no dignity of conscious until there is an acknowledgement that ethical heroism, Christian empathy and youth empowerment are roads less travelled in many of our youth programmes, especially in developed nations.

Finally, while I am a dreamer, I wish it could be said that joining the heroic revolution for Christ will guarantee immediate victory. That is not the case. What is consistent with the Christian tradition is not that God will always save us when acting heroically in love, but that God will always be with us when we stand with proper conviction. In that vein, though we may fail, Christ will prevail.

It is true that David stood courageously with only a slingshot and his faith in God and won against the giant Goliath; but do not forget Stephen, who preached God's message directly to the Sanhedrin and was stoned. Daniel receives high regard for surviving an all-night ordeal with lions whom God had given lockjaw; yet John the Baptist, who was given the heroic privilege of announcing the coming of Christ, was beheaded. The three Hebrew boys Shadrach, Meshach and Abednego were recovered unsinged after being cast into a fiery furnace; but Jesus, the Son of God, had to die on a cross in order to heroically save us all.

We must move towards the day when youth programmes tremble no more before social acts of greatness for Christ. When this happens, evangelistic social action may prove itself as the best, most liberating tool for youth groups participating in the worldwide revolution of God. May your young people respond affirmatively when presented with the heroic question, 'Whom shall I send, and who will go for us?' May they, like Isaiah, respond with great zeal, 'Here am I Lord, send me!' Either way, some will step forward – they will be all you need to begin – who do not fear to make a stand for Jesus, and who muster the moral determination to say, 'O drug user, O pimp, O pusher, O prostitute, O rip-off business, O wicked political representative, O racist, O sexist, O apathetic church member, pastor, youth worker, we will no longer allow you to do business as usual any longer without proactive resistance from the heroic people of God. We have come to say, with the three Hebrew boys and with Esther, 'Our God is able to save us from anything you do to us', but even if he does not, we want you to know we will never support what you do. 'If we perish, let us perish.'[40]

CHAPTER 6

Salt or Semtex? Does Church-based Youthwork Reinforce Prejudice in Northern Ireland?

ANN DICKSON

> See to it that no one takes you captive through hollow and deceptive philosophy, which depends on human tradition and the basic principles of this world rather than on Christ.
>
> (Colossians 2.8, NIV)

Salt or Semtex?

Church workers tend to optimistically believe they are doing some good – preaching the word, sharing God's love, being 'salt in the world' – and undoubtedly there is a lot of good work being done in the name of Christianity. When we stand apart from the Church, however, and consider its overall role in many parts of the world, the picture is less rosy. This paper considers the negative impact of the established churches in one country whose churches remain central to the life of its people and yet is renowned for its never-ending conflict. I shall be presenting the preliminary findings of research regarding the role of Christian youth workers in 'cross-community' work and reflecting on the riches of the other findings concerned with the role of the Church in Northern Ireland. The main question being, 'does church-based youthwork reinforce prejudice in Northern Ireland?'

In this paper I hope to do the following.

- Outline the role that the established churches play in the Northern Ireland conflict. Offer the contention that the common theology and church practices often reinforce prejudice and sectarianism.
- Consider how church-based youth workers who are currently involved in cross-community work became involved in establishing that work. I hope to show that the established churches are, at best, a weak support for reconciliation, at worst, a barrier to community relations, but almost never a catalyst for change within Christian youth workers who have initiated community relations work.
- Suggest some implications for the training of church-based youth workers and offer some signs of hope that the Protestant established churches are beginning to take the issue of cross-community work seriously.

Background Information Regarding the Role of the Church in Northern Ireland

One would think, after the many years of civil war in a country that possesses one of the highest concentrations of church attendees in Europe, that by now there would be plentiful examples of how the established churches have rallied to build bridges between the two traditions.

While it is true that there are many examples of good practice of cross-community contact pioneered by individual Christians or parachurch organizations, it has been difficult to research models of good practice of cross-community work (including youthwork) between established churches in Northern Ireland. The scarcity of such interchurch youth programmes has been sorely apparent.

Christ called his followers to be peacemakers and yet it is to our shame that we live in a country where the clearest dividing line between the protagonists of the conflict is religion, and that religion is so easily entangled in the everyday violence. One could easily argue that the Church is essentially linked to the violence and any attempt at reconciliation at a structural level has been too weak and too late. Throughout history it has generally supported intolerance, superiority and sectarian systems of domination both directly and indirectly. The church is also guilty of sins of omission – not doing enough to build spaces of trust and reconciliation in the chaos of society. The Church's own submission to the Opsahl Commission gave 'some indication of the record – good and bad, successful and failed, encouraging and depressing – of the churches in Northern Ireland over the last quarter of a century of strife. There has been concern; there has been action of different kinds but there is still an alarming amount to be accomplished.'[1]

There are many examples of how the Church has ensured that its influence is clearly imprinted directly or indirectly on the organization of society via the political arena, healthcare, employment and education. There may well be positive aspects to this process, but it is also true that its influence adds to the segregation of society. For example, the education system has been organized in such a way that, generally, Protestants go to the state schools and Catholics attend the 'maintained' schools. It is interesting to note, however, that there have been some changes recently in the thinking about the usefulness of this strategy, and that even within the Catholic clergy, who traditionally supported separate schooling, there is now widespread support for integrated education.[2]

The practice of religion often has indirect and unintentional consequences. As a Community Relations Worker with the YMCA, I was often disappointed to note that the major practical blockage to an interchurch group arranging activities was the difficulty of finding an evening free to meet together. For those who are highly committed to church life, church activities can take up a lot of energy. The Norwegian anthropologist Larsen noted, 'it is possible to be occupied every evening of the week with some sort of church work, and very many people are'.[3]

Therefore, the churches provide important social networks for their own people and contribute to the practice of socializing with their 'own kind', reinforcing the fact that most people live in segregated areas and have been educated in a segregated school system.[4] Prejudice is often reinforced by ignorance and lack of positive contact. It is easy to believe the myths and fears of your ancestors when you do not meet people from a different religious tradition and interpret the current political events through the eyes of your own isolated perceptions.

The Role of the Clergy

Even today, after nearly 30 years of conflict, most ministers see their role primarily as a pastoral one, being caught up in the business of 'looking after their flock', and not as one of being agents of change for peace-building in the local community.[5] Generally the churches are perceived as being supporters of the sectarian status quo, not as neutral peacemakers or workers for justice for all groups in society. For example, there are plenty of Protestant clergy willing to support the Orange Lodge church services that are largely seen as antagonistic to the Catholic community. They are partisan; keepers of their denomination.

This is hardly surprising, given that some theological colleges are only now beginning to facilitate students to understand the community relations issues. The clergy who do step out to build bridges with 'the other side' are taking enormous risks, for it would not be the first time that a Kirk session blocks an intercommunity meeting or a minister finds himself isolated from his own congregation. For, although the heads of the main churches support interchurch meetings and have been associated with calls for an end to violence, 'there have never been major changes in the pattern of church relationships',[6] nor have there been the structures in place for this to happen in the local community. The onus has been on individual clergy who are so motivated that they will take the risks to set up cross-community initiatives.[7] However, there are recent signs of hope, which we will discuss later.

Does Our Common Theology Reinforce Prejudice?

Despite the fact that most people in Northern Ireland do not consider the Northern Irish conflict to be essentially about theology,[8] it is, in fact, arguable that the common theology and practice of Christianity have added fuel to the fire in the conflict. The predominant theology is evangelical in nature, which tends to emphasize personal salvation, perhaps to the cost of positive social action, tolerance and listening to different views. Concerning themselves with building up the individual's spirituality, the churches have generally been slow to react to injustices in the community, afraid to take a radical step in building bridges between the two communities and suspicious that building trust and understanding between the different churches could be viewed as dangerous ecumenism.

Although most church attendees would not describe themselves as fundamentalist, the fundamentalist influence is reflected in the political arena. It is hard to compromise when you believe God is on your side and any such action is weakness or even sin. As S. Bruce observes in his study of the popularity of the extremist views of Paisley, 'The Northern Ireland conflict is a religious conflict. Economic and social differences are also crucial, but it was the fact that the competing populations in Ireland adhered and still adhere to competing religious traditions which has given the conflict its enduring and intractable quality. This is the only conclusion that makes sense to Ian Paisley's career . . . his political success can only be understood if one appreciates the central role which evangelical religion plays in Ulster Unionism.'[9]

At a theological conference held in 1996 aimed at Protestant evangelicals,[10] it was observed that many participants were more interested in defending articles of doctrine that make reconciliation difficult for Protestants than they were in working at practical ways of improving community relations. This personal observation is supported by D. Morrow's contention – 'From our research, it is clear that theological reflection by many clergy is focused on defence of clear doctrine rather than on repentance and change. In most theological thinking, there is a clear assumption that change, whether political or theological, has to be undertaken by "the others first". "The problem" is usually located in the doctrines, attitudes and actions of the others, whoever they may be.' The corollary of this is that the speaker is always unable to act, because the other has to change first. 'We are represented towards each other by rival self-righteousness', as Frank Wright wrote, 'and any awareness that the other has reason to fear us is concealed from view.'

Theology permeates our thinking on a subconscious level whether we like it or not. Messages of superiority and 'being on the right side' support the acts of violence that the Church does not support. For the boy throwing a stone at people of another religious denomination, he presumably does not believe God is telling him to do it, but he probably has been given a clear message that he is on the right side. The churches have not been clearly heard to be saying that all violence is wrong. As Morrow suggests, 'the churches are caught up in the spiral of violence, with people identifying the violence against their side.'[11] Religion is often consciously used as a justification for violence even in today's society. Those who defined themselves in a recent Social Attitudes survey as 'strongly religious' were more likely to use religion to support violence, with 20 per cent from the Protestant religion and 30 per cent of the Catholic religion supporting violence with their theology. Of course, this justification is misguided and denounced by the present church leaders. Nevertheless, it could be said that the churches' role in the conflict has historically been interwoven with the violence and, even today, there has been little change in interchurch relationships for condemnation to be taken seriously.

This situation is not unique to Northern Ireland. If we can lose a little of our introspectiveness, which is a trait common in Northern Ireland, and consider South Africa, for example, we can compare their struggle and the role of the Dutch Reformed Church in supporting a system of apartheid. However, there are other factors that facilitated the political changes in South Africa, including the quality of leadership in several of the key players in the political process who believed in non-violence, the integrity of taking risks for the sake of justice and the ability to inspire the mass of the people. As yet, we do not possess this vital component.[12]

Does Youth Ministry Reflect the Churches' Ministry?

This paper, however, is primarily concerned with the role of the established churches and their support or hindrance of church-based youth workers trying to build trust and understanding in the local community. Does youth ministry reflect the Church's pastoral role? Over the last three years, liaising with the Protestant youth departments and through the work of Youth Link, visiting many youth groups, I believe it is fair to state that most of the church-based youthwork is primarily pastoral and social in its nature and generally the practice of youth ministry reflects the Church's ministry in Northern Ireland.

Overall, it seems Protestant church-based youthwork does not present a radical picture of innovative cross-community work. Many Catholic church youth centres are in partnership with the Education Board and find themselves automatically involved in some sort of cross-community contact. There are fewer Protestant church youth centres in that scenario because, historically, the Protestant churches were more independent from the Education Board situation. There are a few innovative projects that have just recently been established, such as the PACT project in Lurgan and the Barnabas Centre in Enniskillen, which was established by the Methodist Church and is now operating as a cross-community project.

The vast majority of peace-building work has been initiated by secular groups or parachurch groups, such as reconciliation groups that may have Christian members, or youth groups which have a Christian ethos similar to the YMCA, or community groups which have as participants people who may be church members. It seems that the churches like playing safe or reconciliation work is seemingly not a priority. So, it has been left to other agencies to take risks in developing innovative cross-community programmes.

Some Reasons Protestant Church Youth Workers Gave for Avoiding Facilitating Significant Cross-community Programmes and What These Mean

Our priority is to pass on sound biblical teaching, not to get involved in politics.

I don't feel confident. I would be afraid of opening up a can of worms and not knowing what to do with it.

We've never done it.

It's dangerous . . . we don't want our children marrying the other kind and losing their faith.

We're already too busy.

I don't think some people in the Church would like that sort of thing.

We sent some kids away to America with some Catholic kids but sure it doesn't change anything.

There is some truth in the last statement – personal reconciliation work does *not* change the political situation unless the numbers of people involved in experiences that reduce prejudice and promote trust in the community increase sufficiently. Perhaps then a significant shift in the defensiveness of the political stalemate can take place. It is false to assume that politics is impervious to community relationships. Good political dialogue rests on community stability. Moreover, surely Christians should act out of sense of integrity to God's word, not depending on guaranteed success or ease of expediency?

It seems that the Church's youthwork is perceived to be ineffective – either not doing enough to decrease the political tensions or having even reinforced the existing prejudices by condoning messages of theological superiority and intolerance for those who do not belong to the same religious tradition. We do not find it easy to listen to different theological or political views and the hyperactive treadmills of the Church's youth organizations do not encourage mixing with people from 'the other side'. Young people who marry people from the other religious tradition often find themselves alienated or even persecuted. Too often Church youthwork is not a radical force that challenges the sectarianism of the country, but, rather, either 'ignores' it, complies with it or actually reinforces it. Generally the Church's youthwork does little to challenge sectarianism and the few examples there are of positive community relations work established by a church group are drops in the ocean.

Given that the Church generally reflects the sectarianism of society and that we have not been overwhelmed by dynamic interchurch activities to mention, it may be worthy to study Protestant Christians who are actually currently facilitating cross-community work. What motivated these youth workers to do this? What was the role the Church played in their motivation for this work?

Findings from Interviews with Protestant Christians Involved in Cross-community Work

During a period of three months I interviewed Protestant youth workers currently involved in cross-community work. I was interested to explore the processes of change for youth workers who were brought up within the evangelical Protestant tradition in Northern Ireland and, despite all the barriers to cross-community work and the lack of real structural support within the churches for reconciliation work, nevertheless facilitated cross-community work with young people. The research done in this area compares the processes of change of Christians who are now involved in cross-community work and the findings of Dr Mari Fitzduff who studied the processes of change within people who had participated in violence and who now no longer did.

Her research identifies the 'permission' people need to change their attitudes and the 'contradictions' that effect the change in their mindsets. The permission and contradictions needed are different depending on whether you tend to be a 'thinker' or 'belonger'. I used similar questioning techniques to those used by Dr Fitzduff, although there are additional questions regarding possible theological changes. In reality, there are not many Christians currently involved in facilitating cross-community work, especially in the Protestant established churches. Those interviewed had a variety of backgrounds with diverse experiences of family life. Some participants were raised listening to parental prejudicial remarks, while others were not raised with flagrant sectarian remarks. They came from diverse social and economic backgrounds and a variety of church traditions. Some belonged to the main established churches and others belonged to the smaller denominations or independent churches. Most of those interviewed were not currently working with young people in the main denominations – they found other places to 'follow their vocation'.

Although I am presenting the preliminary findings of my research, the results seem to reflect the general situation perceived by church youth officers, observations by Education Board Youth Department staff and Youth Link staff. A common thread has emerged: the established churches were not the primary catalyst in facilitating cross-community work. It was very rare for any of the Protestant youth workers who belonged to the established churches to recall a sermon that challenged the sectarianism of the land,[13] that called for an end to discrimination against Catholics, for example, or ever really addressed the roots of the conflict in Ireland. It will be interesting to observe if the next generation of youth workers will testify to their churches' sermons and if inter-church activities were a factor in motivating them to facilitate cross-community work.

When one is looking for radical cross-community work between young people crossing the divides, it seems there are very few examples of current, genuine cross-community youth projects initiated within the established churches. It is debatable if these lonely initiatives would continue without the enthusiasm of a few individuals. It seems that most churches need to concentrate on building enthusiasm for cross-community work, addressing their own insecurities, exploring their own identity and planning a strategy for such cross-community work. Most church groups are a long way off actually doing any cross-community work.

Those participants interviewed who are presently involved in cross-community work have not cited the established Church as the main catalyst for change regarding community relations work. Sometimes the church attendees were isolated from the realities of the conflict and the Church did not help them to explore any of the issues of the conflict. Speaking about the 'Troubles', one worker says, 'It was there but, you know, middle-class Holywood, you were removed from the thing. It was out there, it was happening but, at the end of the day, it didn't impact my life.'

At best they have found weak support for their work. For example, one worker commented that the sermons were mainly concerned with pastoral themes:

> You know the Church as a family thing . . . nothing specifically addressed the situation. I suppose the Church talked about the Troubles in a very abstract way, you could maybe relate general themes to how you should treat others but it wasn't specific. Now I'm just trying to see people as people. Ephesians 2 talks about breaking down the dividing wall of hostility . . .

> Well that to me really speaks of the Protestant–Catholic thing in Northern Ireland.

At worst the churches they belong to added barriers to the young people's quest for reconciliation. One youth worker currently working for the YMCA left her voluntary youth work in her family church because she was so shocked at the blatant sectarian statements of the youth worker in charge. Another worker states:

> I find it hard to fathom how a minister of the so-called Gospel can stand up and preach hate . . . and the politics that go with that don't go with my faith . . . I maybe would have been behind him at one stage, you know, but now it's gone the opposite way.

Many of the Protestant youth workers interviewed, although presently working for one of the established churches, found valuable training and community relations experiences in para-churches or non-established house churches. It seems house churches, charismatic churches or a few independent churches are freer to initiate cross-community links.

In talking to the youth workers, I was interested in what was necessary for the attitudes to change. At some point those who changed their attitudes were faced with contradictions:

- as a result of primarily *thinking*, about for example:
  - studying the biblical principles of being salt in society and the implications for Christians of being agents of reconciliation;
  - understanding the political and historical situation and realizing the inherited myths of our religious tradition;

or

- coming into contact with people from another religious tradition, having a sense of belonging to a new group, enjoying the relationships that developed and realizing that the fears and prejudices they were raised with were unjustifiable.

Generally those interviewed moved from conservative political theological thinking to a more inclusive political theological thinking system. They moved from 'seeing everything in black and white' to having the ability to see the complexities of a situation and being able to be relatively content with some uncertainties.

This would reflect Fitzduff's analysis of the processes of change that she observed with ex-paramilitaries, namely that people needed 'contradictions' to their old way of thinking and those contradictions were different depending on whether you tended to be a 'cogitator' or a 'belonger'.

Can Our Traditional Evangelical Influences Reinforce Prejudice?

It is also interesting to look at Fitzduff's descriptions of the characteristics of monistic thinking and wonder whether or not our fundamentalist influences in society can contribute to reinforcing this tendency. For further details of her analysis it is useful to read the conclusions of her thesis. However, in brief, she describes 'monism' as 'Cognitive simplicity, stereotyping, conventional thinking, certainty of beliefs, intolerance of uncertainty, field-dependent thinking, concrete reflection and own values as objective.' Those people who have a mindset characterized by monistic thinking usually use projection and blame to explain situations of conflict. They seem to be certain of their fixed identity, which tends to be ethnocentric.

People who have shifted to pluralistic thinking have cognitive complexity, have a type of uncertainty about beliefs, principled thinking, see their own values as subjective, possess an inclusive identity and are more likely to approach conflict with the attitude of being interested in the process and a win-win approach rather than taking positions and having a win-lose approach.

What, Then, Are the Implications for the Training of Church-based Youth Workers?

For church-based youthwork to be salt in the world, we need the hearts and minds of youth workers to be motivated to take risks, to work in difficult situations, to be willing to take personal criticism and to be misunderstood by perhaps family or friends or even other church people. Our work needs to be as effective as possible, learning what is the most successful way of changing attitudes and not just hoping God will do something without us making much effort.

The churches need to develop a strategy to encourage cross-community work at every level. This includes encouragement, training and support for all church-based youth leaders who are involved in facilitating the cross-community work, and for those churches not involved in cross-community work to give an account of why it has not been possible. There are agencies to help church-based youth workers to become involved in cross-community work, but there seems to be a lack of willingness to establish this work. We have accepted the norm of society rather than expecting the best innovative work to come out of the churches.

However, how do we encourage a real experience rather than tokenism? How do we inspire hearts and minds?

Those currently involved in cross-community work show a zeal that cannot be imposed by a church committee telling people to be involved in cross-community work. They have experienced a life-changing situation and wanted to share that experience with other people. Perhaps that is what we need to concentrate on – ensuring that the Church's youth workers have positive interchurch experiences and supporting them to duplicate experiences for the young people they are working with.

Planning programmes for thinkers and belongers

It seems that it would be essential to develop programmes in our youth ministry that encourage critical thinking processes, discussions and dynamic group experiences. As a result of the interviews with church-based youth workers, it seems it is wise to plan contact with people from different traditions, especially for the 'belongers', making sure the experiences are enjoyable yet challenging, as it has been noted that prejudice is often reinforced by ignorance and lack of positive contact. For those identified as 'thinkers', it may be useful to provide resources and biblical materials for study groups and individuals that would be instrumental in challenging the stereotyping, sectarianism and prejudice that permeates the society and the Church.

Testing real change – testing attitudes and observing behavioural outcomes

With generous governmental and European funds being allocated to cross-community projects, there is a growing call for accountability and evaluation processes. Cynics among us may say that it is easy to produce figures to prove that people have taken part in cross-community projects, but quantitative evaluation methods do not prove that anyone's attitudes have changed. However, there is a growing body of research into appropriate evaluation methods to test attitudinal and behavioural changes in the participants of such projects.

For example, Dr Peter Weinreich[14] offers an interesting model for 'identity structural analysis', with a computer package to supplement the process so that one can identify changes in participants' attitudes, on-going conflicts, levels of tolerance, respect for other traditions and so on. With evaluation methods like this, we hope to find out which are the most effective training programmes for church-based youth workers for increasing tolerance, openness to others and so on. One could also test for behavioural changes. For example, if some young people participated in a cross-community experience you could ask, did their behaviour change as a result of the experience? Have they participated in voluntary follow-up experiences? Do they show fewer signs of prejudice regarding people from different traditions – for example, name-calling? Do they show less avoidance of sensitive issues and more willingness to engage in discussing the political situation?

Church workers could use such evaluation techniques if they really wanted to test people's attitudes instead of hoping that people's hearts have changed. Whether a person's attitudes will remain 'changed' is a further question.

Let us hope and pray that the next generation of church-based youth workers will say that the churches were the main catalyst in their lives for building peace and justice in their community and there are signs of hope.

Signs of Hope

As has been noted, one of the largest blockages to effectiveness has been the lack of a structure to encourage the bulk of churches to be involved in intercommunity contact or cross-community work. There may be signs of change in this area as some churches are initiating structures to encourage interchurch understanding. Whether these structural changes prove to be real catalysts for change, however, remains to be seen.

Approximately two years ago, the Presbyterian Church, the largest Protestant Church, appointed reconciliation agents and it will be interesting to observe how this development will encourage individual churches to initiate 'reconciliation work'. This year, 1997, the main Protestant churches are examining their relationship with the Orange Order, and it seems there are more voices within the main Protestant churches having the courage to state publicly their disapproval of these links with the Orange Order.

There are signs of change regarding youth ministry structures. In 1990, the four main churches – namely the Catholic, Presbyterian, Methodist and Church of Ireland churches – established a training organization for youth workers: Youth Link Northern Ireland. It was later joined by the Religious Society of Friends and the Non-subscribing Presbyterian Church. For the main denominations, to be willing to be seen to be working together is a sign of hope in itself, and then there is the actual work of Youth Link, training youth workers of different denominations together and encouraging cross-community programmes.

There are always glimmers of hope – individual clergy who take risks in setting up initiatives to heal the divisions, who may speak up against injustice against people who are not members of their flock or who encourage the young people in their church to think about the biblical principles of reconciliation, forgiveness and social action. In recent years, the main denominations' leaders have become more outspoken against all violence. There are Christian youth workers from all denominations working inside and outside the main churches who are facilitating cross-community work. There are always a few who will not march to the beat of the ancient drums. Perhaps this trickle will become a torrent of change with the back-up of Church structures and an increasing will within the church to go against the flow.

Conclusion – Finding the Will to do Our Best

Too often, the Church reflects society's norms and protects its own interests instead of following God's teaching regarding forgiveness, reconciliation and concern for all. The Church has been reluctant to make reconciliation work a priority; its pastoral duties seem short-sighted and narrow in their brief. This narrow pastoral brief has been reflected in the youthwork of the established churches, although there are many examples of individual Christians working within parachurch agencies that encourage cross-community programmes. It takes courage to initiate cross-community work and church workers need support, proper structures for accountability and encouragement from the clergy and laity of the Church. There are also practical lessons to be learned from the secular world, including how we can benefit from research into the effectiveness of some community relations work. We should be as 'wise as serpents', arming ourselves with all the help from various sources we can find so that we can do our best instead of reacting with a weak-willed response to the sectarianism of the country.

CHAPTER 7

Iconoclasm: Shattering the Mindset of 'Ethnic Minority' Youthwork

ANNA CHAKKO-GEORGE

A Note About Terminology

In Britain, it is common practice to use the term 'ethnic minority' to define those people or groups who are not the dominant majority in terms of their ethnicity. I have reservations about the use of this term as a label, and prefer to use the term 'black'. I shall, however, use the terms 'black' and 'ethnic minority' – or the more preferable 'minority ethnic' – interchangeably.

The term 'black' itself has several meanings and applications, and I shall use it in different ways in the course of this paper. In general, I shall use 'black' as a general label for all people who would not define themselves as 'white' in terms of their ethnic identity. An exception to this is where I make the distinction between Asian and African or African-Caribbean, where 'black' may be used in reference to the latter.

In Britain, the term 'Asian' generally, and inaccurately, refers to those from the Indian subcontinent; I have rather shamefully adopted such usage for the sake of brevity in this paper. The term 'African-Caribbean' is used to refer specifically to those people from the West Indies whose ancestors originally came from Africa.

Introduction

The situation of Asian girls growing up in Britain represents a unique challenge for the Church. Girls socialized in one culture at home encounter another in the wider community. Tensions, misunderstandings and frustrations are commonplace and yet this situation is rich in intercultural and inter-religious contact and communication.

Young people from different cultural and ethnic groups are growing up together in many of our cities and towns. Cross-cultural friendships are commonplace. The Church needs to respond both to the problems faced by these young people as well as to the richness their friendships represent. As a context for sensitive mission, those involved in youth ministry need to take seriously the question of how to engage appropriately with these mixed groups while remaining faithful to the Gospel.

In this paper, I shall examine the needs of young people from minority ethnic groups by means of a case study of Asian girls. I shall then look at the traditional response of 'ethnic minority youth-work', in order to critique the extent to which those needs are, or are not, being addressed. I will go on to propose an alternative model for youthwork, using a pilot conference called Iconoclast as a case study. Finally, the strengths and weaknesses of that model will be used to shed further light on both the needs of young people from minority ethnic groups and on an appropriate response.

Reflections on a Case Study of Asian Girls: What are the Needs of Young People from Minority Ethnic Groups?

Working alongside Asian girls in their culturally mixed peer groups in two different schools, two issues have demanded attention again and again, namely *identity* and *assimilation*. The different cultural context of each school raised different thoughts and perspectives on these issues and their significance for youth ministry in this context.

School A

This school had a large percentage of Asian girls, almost all of whom were Asian Muslims. They tended to stay in all-Asian groups. Racism was evident in institutionalized, blatant policies, and in the relationship between the Asian girls and the rest of the school.

'I'm not English, I'm not Pakistani, so what am I?'

Working with Asian Muslim girls in this school exposed the fact that they were consciously (as well as subconsciously) struggling to find some resolution to this question of identity. They were wrestling with the question, 'where do I, as a second generation Pakistani Muslim girl, fit into "British" society?' On the one hand, they felt a strong allegiance to their faith and culture in terms of the identity it gave them, which felt true to where they were coming from. On the other hand, their desire to express another part of themselves, and to enjoy the same freedom as their peers, meant they rebelled in various ways against parental pressure to conform to their Asian culture.

The few white girls who were part of their relationship groups did not appear to be asking any questions as a result of their friendships with girls from this very different cultural background. They weren't asking themselves, 'what does it mean for us when we talk about Britain as a multicultural society?' or 'will understanding who *she* is help me understand who *I* am differently?' Shared conversation invariably took place according to a white agenda in terms of music, dance, film, careers, boys, fashion and so on.

Their strong religious and (closely tied) cultural differences, against a backdrop of institutionalized racism, made the Muslim girls' struggle for identity a more necessary part of their existence. This need to struggle for 'self' resulted in a psychological and sociological sense of separateness. The white girls, as the power base was theirs, did not feel this same 'need' to work out their identity in the light of their culturally mixed friendships. Separateness was recognized but understood as being an 'Asian problem' as 'they're the ones who are different'. Yet, in many ways, this 'Asian problem' served as an 'Asian strength' in their struggle for identity, for selfhood and against assimilation.

School B

This school has far fewer Asian girls. These girls are predominantly Asian Christians, dispersed in culturally mixed groups. Racism in the school is most often experienced as colour blindness, although this itself is a thin and peeling veneer.

The Asian girls at School B are, generally speaking, part of culturally mixed friendship groups to a much greater extent than the Asian girls at School A, who, for the most part, were in all-Asian friendship groups. While this may seem to be a much healthier, more positive state of affairs, a closer understanding of the group suggests that the Asian girls at School B are denied, by the scope of their peer groups, any opportunity to express their cultural identity.

> What does it profit a person if they gain the whole world but lose their very self? (Matthew 16.26)[1]

The Asian girls at School B, mostly from Christian family backgrounds, seem not to be engaged in the conscious 'thinking through' of their identity that was true of the Asian Muslim girls at School A. There is not the same sense of struggle because they have learnt to make 'fitting in' second nature. They value integration at any cost, even the loss of their identity. It is more important to belong to the mainstream than to gain recognition of their own culture (which is not necessarily the same as their parents' culture). They seem almost reluctant to acknowledge their 'Asian-ness', let alone explore it for themselves.

This is reminiscent of the Australian government's policy of assimilation, which came into force in the 1920s and was ruthlessly implemented for some 40 years. Aboriginal children were separated from their families by force and placed with white foster parents. The idea was that they would be reared as whites and then the lifestyle, culture and, eventually, the very racial existence of the Aboriginal people would be successfully wiped out. In a sense, the Asian girls' solution to integration, to fitting in, is as potentially culturally damaging as that Aboriginal holocaust. It may not be government policy, but it is important to ask why it is that Asian young people are choosing this kind of cultural oblivion. Is it free choice or tactical survival, given the uneven playing field?

Coming from a Christian background may have made it easier for many of these Asian girls to 'fit in' with Western society, as their Christianity will have taught and allowed them to separate religion from culture. (Their parents or grandparents were converted to Christianity from another religion, and, very probably, were taught to leave anything that had cultural ties with their old faith behind. Their old faith came to be seen as part of their 'culture', that consequently was considered to be clearly separate from and irreconcilable with their new Christian faith.) So they can go into school with the parts of themselves that fit, and leave the parts that don't – their Asian culture and, ironically, also their Christianity – at home. This cannot be the wholeness promised in Christ.

This desire to get on, fit in and somehow belong in the mainstream of British society has meant that these Asian girls have chosen to accept an identity given to them by the dominant culture over and above self-worth and cultural integrity. The cost of integration has been assimilation and, with it, the danger of an irreversible loss of cultural wholeness.

Perhaps the danger for the Asian Muslim girls, on the other hand, is that a resolution of the struggle may be found in allegiance to their inherited faith and cultural identity at the expense of a participative and formative say in British society, of which they are, at least in terms of their civil rights, a part. Alternatively, a danger may lie in the choice that some have made – rejection of the whole Asian cultural package and a wholehearted embrace of Western culture at the expense of roots, history and their God-given Asian identity.

From an examination of the contexts of these Asian girls, it is evident that there is a specific need for youthwork that empowers black young people to arrive at a positive cultural identity, which is not one prescribed by the dominant culture. This identity should not have to be one that is bought at the price of cultural integrity, nor of full and equal participation in society. Hence, there is also the need for youthwork that promotes the opportunity for black young people to express this cultural identity in societal life, which means challenging prejudice and racism in the mindset of the dominant culture.

The Response of 'Traditional' Ethnic Minority Youthwork

Most statutory bodies now recognize the inequality of opportunity that exists in most areas of civic life for people from minority ethnic groups, and have adopted policies that seek to address this in their practice. Racism is becoming widely recognized as one of the key issues to be covered in informal education, or youthwork, practice. Consequently, many urban youth service agencies, both statutory and voluntary, have an 'ethnic minorities' team, worker or project.

The Oxfordshire County Council Youth Service has an ethnic minorities team, which has recently been renamed The Asian and African-Caribbean Youth Project. The Project's Annual Report 1996 states: 'The purpose of our work is to involve black young people in youth provision which allows them to explore issues that affect and surround them, including culture, tradition, identity and positive images.'[2]

This recognition of the need for appropriate, culturally specific provision (or, in our case, ministry) for young people from minority cultures is crucially important. Historical inequalities, daily experiences of discrimination, verbal and physical attacks, struggle with cultural identity, negative self-images created by racial stereotyping and prejudice – all this is part of the racist experience of black young people. Culturally specific youth ministry is necessary in order for the self-understanding of these young people to become positive – informed from a perspective that challenges, rather than being simply a reinforcement of, the dominant white cultural view. It underpins any work in this context that seeks to be 'wholistic', which addresses the social as well as the spiritual needs of black young people.

Failure to recognize and provide for cultural differences institutionalizes racism; white cultural dominance becomes structural, part of the set-up of the youth ministry. 'Colour blind' ministries are visually and intellectually impaired ministries, as well as being impairing or disabling ministries, for if cultural difference is made illegitimate, then the ability to own, explore and express one's cultural identity is lost. 'Colour blind' ministries are also 'prophetically impaired' ministries – they are unable to declare God's will against injustice, oppression and inequality as they can neither see beyond nor speak into a situation of which they are intrinsically a part.

This failure to perceive injustice and therefore effect change is evidenced in many areas where such 'colour blind' policies are in practice, a fact noted in the 1996 OFSTED report on the achievements of pupils from minority ethnic groups in schools in the United Kingdom:

> Failure to address ethnic diversity has proved counter-productive at the school level. Where schools have adopted 'colour blind' policies, for example, inequalities of opportunity have been seen to continue. In contrast, research has begun to examine the benefits of addressing diversity as an important and changing part of school life.[3]

Remarkably, the emphasis in the Church's activity – often in attempting to address issues of racism – has been on ignoring ethnicity for the sake of unity. Recognizing cultural difference and the need for culturally specific ministry, let alone addressing it, is a rare and endangered practice in the arena of Christian youth ministry. It is necessary for those engaged in youth ministry, if not for the Church as a whole, to learn from models in the secular youthwork field. This is not to encourage an imitating or copying mentality (one that, sadly, is already too common in Church culture and youth ministry), but to engage with and critique such models in order to improve our practice as youth ministers.

Critique

Many towns and cities, as well as rural areas, have some degree of statutory youth service provision. This may be in the form of youth clubs, information services, detached youthwork, sports projects, music and arts projects, homelessness projects and so on. In towns and cities where there are notable percentages of people from minority ethnic groups, and where sufficient budget resources are allocated, a youth service may also set up an 'ethnic minorities' worker or team to specifically explore issues of culture, identity and so on that are relevant to the ethnicity of the young people concerned.

The focus on culture found in this 'traditional' model of 'ethnic minority' youthwork provides a forum for black young people in which the cultural agenda is recognized as an ongoing one. Themes such as race, culture, ethnicity and identity are addressed as 'black' issues, that is, issues important for the self-understanding and struggle of people from minority ethnic groups.

There is, in practice, a serious problem with this traditional structure or model of work with young people from minority ethnic groups: it is a problem of marginalization. This happens on several levels. First, this model marginalizes the marginalized – the very people it seeks to serve. In removing the exploration of issues concerned with culture and ethnicity to the 'ethnic minorities team' or 'the Asian and African-Caribbean youth project', they become solely 'black' or 'Asian' problems or concerns. This reinforces the racist perception that the dominant white world view is the 'norm', and that words or phrases like 'ethnic' and 'cultural background' only apply to 'them'. Racism is, of course, recognized as an issue that may need to be one of the topics covered in the mainstream youth service provision, such as in youth club discussions with young people (along with AIDS awareness, drugs education and so on!) as 'it can be a problem in inner city areas'.

An event from my own practice as an intercultural youth worker serves as a good case study on this point.

Case Study

In November 1996, I found myself in the midst of a situation of racial conflict at the local school where I work. I had got to know an Asian girl – I shall call her Susan – and her group of friends. The four other girls in this group were all black. Susan and her group were threatening to fight an Irish boy – I shall call him Ryan – who had allegedly made strongly racist remarks to Susan. This, the girls informed me, was the latest in a stream of racist behaviour towards Susan and others.

The atmosphere had reached fever pitch, with a by now large group of black girls on one side and an even larger group of white (many of them Irish) boys a short distance away on the other, venting anger, hurling abuse and threatening to erupt into a physical fight at any moment.

I was asked to intervene by one of the Asian girls present. I suggested that it would be easier to resolve the situation if we could ascertain exactly what had gone on by talking to the two individuals concerned.

I started by talking to Ryan on his own, away from the group. He was very upset, almost tearful, and adamant that he wasn't 'a racist'. He explained that although some of his friends often used racist language and had shouted racist names at the girls, he did not participate. He did not want to point the finger at a mate, but neither did he want to be accused of racism. He agreed to apologize for anything that he may have said or done that might have unintentionally caused offence.

I then talked to Susan, explaining what Ryan had told me. I asked her if she could be sure that the insult had come from Ryan and not another member of his group. She could not be certain, and although it did not take away the fact that one of the group had thrown the insult, she agreed to accept an apology from Ryan.

After the apology had been made, I got into a conversation with Susan and her group of friends. It was one of those ground-breaking dialogues in which my relationship with the girls suddenly went a lot deeper as we talked honestly and at length about our experiences of racism, and the girls shared feelings they were unable to express to others in school. One of them said, 'but you know what it's like, sometimes you can't take it any more, you just want to fight back'. I went on to explain that fighting back is important, but that sometimes physical fighting doesn't help get the message across – it simply reinforces the stereotype and feeds prejudiced perceptions.

I was extremely pleased with what was a great piece of youth-work. I had prevented a fight in a constructive way. I had managed to talk to both parties about how they were feeling and how they saw the situation. Ryan had apologized to Susan and Susan had, on one level, accepted his apology. I had opened up discussion with the girls on a level that deepened our relationship, and we had explored issues of race, culture and identity. An excellent example of what my role as Intercultural Project Worker is all about – *and* all in the space of a 45-minute school lunch break!

Susan and her group have not talked to me again since that day. On reflection, I can see some of the reason for this. On one level, the girls may have seen my actions in preventing a fight as aligning myself with the teachers/school authorities. Fights are one of the highlights of school breaks, and I had effectively stolen their thunder. Underlying this, though, is a more serious message. The girls, all of whom were from minority ethnic groups, saw the fight as a way of making themselves heard and their feelings acknowledged in a white arena. Talking to another black or Asian person about their feelings and frustrations was fine, perhaps even valuable, but those feelings remained marginalized – unvoiced and invisible – from their white peers. For me, the conversation was so much more valuable than a fight, but to the girls it may have been ultimately worthless.

Second, the traditional structure or model of 'ethnic minority' youthwork marginalizes the youth worker. Most youthwork agencies operate under a particular framework in terms of youthwork practice. Staff discussions and critique of youthwork practice will centre on this framework and its generic application. The 'ethnic minorities' project worker has to make the necessary 'translation' of this thinking to apply it to the particular cultural context in which they are working (Asian, black, Chinese) as a solitary activity. This leads to a sense of isolation, both of the work and of the worker.

Finally, this model marginalizes the thinking. From the thinking done by black young people in their exploration of their personal and historical experience, to the thinking done by the youth worker on cultural identity arising from their work in that context, the lessons to be learnt and applied by *all* young people in today's multicultural society remain sidelined from the 'mainstream', important research for specialists in the field, but seemingly irrelevant for general youthwork practice.

The traditional model of 'ethnic minority' youthwork is that it aims to provide a service that addresses the specific culture and needs of black young people. It understands the value of such a focus in redressing the inequalities of generic statutory provision. However, the marginalization of black groups and their issues from the mainstream of British social concern and activity, becomes part of the mindset of such youthwork strategy. More than this, it ignores the need to understand and address 'culture' and 'ethnicity' in the dominant white arena, and to recognize the contribution that those from black groups can make to this understanding.

Racism is tackled at a personal education level, even at policy level, but it remains institutionalized as long as the challenges to *all*, presented by those from minority ethnic groups, are marginalized as 'black' or 'minority' concerns rather than a British concern.

All young people need to come to an understanding of their identity – that is part of the process of adolescence, the achievement of selfhood. A 'wholistic' understanding of this identity achievement should include the positive embracing of one's cultural identity, although it is becoming increasingly difficult to work out what that might be. T. Modood, S. Beishon and S. Virdee, in their research studies into ethnic minority identities, conclude:

> . . . ethnic identity, far from being some primordial stamp upon an individual, is a plastic and changing badge of membership. Ethnic identity is a product of a number of forces: social exclusion and stigma and political resistance to them, distinctive cultural and religious heritages as well as new forms of culture, communal and familial loyalties, marriage practices, coalition of interests and so on. Hence the boundaries of groups are unclear and shifting, especially when groups seek to broaden an ethnic identity or to accommodate membership in a number of overlapping groups. And this leaves out the broader social, economic and political forces.[4]

For black people, it is important that an understanding of this identity should not be one that has been prescribed for them by the dominant white culture. Positive identity achievement, which includes the resolution and understanding of ethnic identity, is also necessary for young people from the dominant white culture. This is important not only in terms of their personal development, but also in terms of their positive participation in society – that is, if they are to question their taught history and change the entrenched power base, to move from defensive action or inaction that arises from guilt, to positive action that arises from a sense of their responsibility as the powerholders.

When relational youthwork is understood in terms of practising Christian Relational Care,[5] it becomes more than simply building relationships in order to be a friend to young people. These relationships provide an opportunity to understand the particular needs of different groups of young people, and to respond by cooperating with God's mission in the world: witnessing the whole Gospel to the whole person in their whole context. Addressing this need for self-identity and a positive, actively multicultural community has to be part of that witness.

What, then, might be a suitable model for such a youth ministry, given that a 'colour blind' model is, at best, inappropriate and, at worst, racist, and that the traditional model of 'ethnic minority' youthwork is inadequate and shortsighted?

The Iconoclast Conference – An Example of Multicultural Youthwork Practice

> I decided many years ago to invent myself. I had obviously been invented by someone else – by a whole society – and I didn't like their invention. Maya Angelou[6]

In February 1996, I invited 18 young women (who I had come to know as a result of youthwork in a local school) to comprise a working party called Iconoclast for two days, exploring their own cultural identity and their collective experience of living in a multicultural society. The girls were 'representatives' from Asian, European and African-Caribbean backgrounds. (In the end, only ten girls were allowed to come as it was held as a residential weekend away.) Each group had a facilitator from their own 'race'. Work was undertaken individually, in race-specific groups and as a whole group.

I would like to focus on a series of three sessions from the Iconoclast Conference as an example of a methodology of multicultural youthwork that offers an alternative to the marginalizing model of traditional 'ethnic minority youthwork' practice. The three sessions were entitled 'I Am', 'Hearing Other Voices', and 'Am I Receiving You?'

I Am

In this session, the young people met in their individual race groups with their facilitator, and tape-recorded 30 minutes of conversation. Each facilitator had the same list of six topics, ranging from food to parents to what it meant to be 'Asian', 'white' or 'black' (depending on the group). Every five minutes, the facilitator would give the group a new topic to talk about.

I facilitated the Asian group. For that group, just having the opportunity to talk together about their 'Asianness' was a new experience. Interestingly, the Asian girl who was always at the centre of things in every conversation at school said little over the weekend. The exception to this was when the girls divided into their race groups – it was only when she was in the company of Asians alone, and not in front of her other friends, that she felt able to talk openly of her 'Asianness'. As the Asian girls started talking, they became more and more excited and positive about their culture, even while being honest about its bad points. They began to own their experience as part of their identity, moving from unease and embarrassment to self-esteem and pride.

Hearing Other Voices

In this session, the three groups listened to the recording of another group, so the Asian group heard that of the black girls; the black group heard that of the white girls; and the white group heard that of the Asian girls. While listening, everyone in each group had to write their comments and questions on a large piece of paper.

The young people's ability to engage with the material, and the tremendous impact it had on them, albeit in different ways, was related to the fact that they had just done the same exercise themselves. If they had not talked about the same subjects themselves just beforehand, they would have heard the tapes very differently. The exercise highlighted the fact that each group had a different perspective on the same topics, and that those differences and perspectives were in some way related to culture and ethnic identity.

Am I Receiving You?

In this session, the three groups came back together as a large group to feed back on the tape they had listened to. Feedback was taken in turns. The group being discussed could not respond until the feedback was over, and then its members had to be heard without interruption. After this, discussion was open to all. Obviously this session needed strong chairing! Some rules were made clear at the outset. For example, each person spoke for themselves, not for the whole race group, and everyone had the right to be heard, however extreme their opinion.

This session got very heated! This was largely because of the honesty with which perceptions were aired, and questions were asked and answered. For example, some of the white girls asked, quite genuinely, clearly feeling affronted but certainly intending no malice, 'If you think of India as home and you like it so much, why don't you just go back home to India?'

For the black girls, the exercise proved to be something of a revelation, as they had been brought up to believe that Asians were 'dirty', 'strange people with strange ways' and to be avoided. It was in this session that the black girls and the Asian girls were able to share and explore their discovery of a lot of common ground, such as behaviour expected at home, experience of church, respect for elders, attitudes to food, experience of racism. The black girls discovered that, in fact, their own experiences identified closely with those of the Asian girls, both in terms of their felt oppression and their tensions/struggles with their inherited culture. Hence, this revelation was two-fold: it was a discovery both of a commonality of experience and values, and that their racial prejudice was something they had been 'taught' by their parents. As a result, they began to form an alliance. The white girls suddenly found themselves isolated, and received the most direct confrontation for their views.

The white girls were now on unfamiliar territory. They were still in the majority in terms of numbers, but quickly sensed that they were the minority (at the Conference) who were not the victims of oppression, but, rather, a part of the culture responsible for it. They found it difficult to acclimatize to this shift in the power base, which became more marked as the Asian and black voices of the oppressed began to resonate together. Although they came from a variety of different backgrounds – Italian, English, and so on – they understood their identity as 'white', with little or no reference to their particular cultural heritage. Yet, unlike those in the other groups, these girls struggled to identify what it meant to be 'white' in any positive sense, and to associate feelings with their racial identity – that is, to describe what it felt like to be 'white'.

The weekend highlighted to the young women the point that friendship in their culturally mixed groups need not, and in fact should not, take place only on the level of the lowest common cultural denominator. They discovered that although many of them had known each other for years and were close friends, they still knew very little about each other or, more accurately, the Asian girls and the black girls knew much more about their white friends' lives than vice versa. Allowing their friendships to be based and governed according to a 'white' agenda was limiting the potential richness of their relationships. They also began to realize that whenever they allow that to happen they reinforce the oppression of those from 'minority' cultures, which as often as not meant themselves.

For the Asian girls in particular the Conference was a space that allowed them to glimpse wholeness in their relationships, and to own a part of their identity that had hitherto been considered unacceptable. For some of the black girls, it was their first significant contact with Asian girls. For all of them, the experience challenged their prejudice and gave new understanding to their relationships in society. The black girls saw no separation between their understanding of their identity and their understanding of and struggle for justice, which was, in different ways, an education for the Asian girls and the white girls. The Conference was an eye-opener for the white girls, not only because they had a glimpse of these different cultures, but also because they saw the hurt and injustice their friends lived with on a daily basis. Moreover, these girls had never before consciously reflected on their culture as being one of many cultures as opposed to 'the norm'.

The Iconoclast Conference was a success. It provided an exciting, challenging and empowering environment for the participants. Their existing friendships were enriched by the process of exploring their cultural diversity and experiencing wholeness in their relationships.

As a methodology for youthwork with young people from minority ethnic groups, it presents, in many ways, a more 'wholistic' approach, as the agenda of cultural identity is worked with as a multicultural and intercultural concern. The model allows mutuality of learning as cultural identity is explored in both its personal and societal application, both in race-specific groups and as a shared endeavour.

I would like to introduce briefly one of the Asian girls who came to the Iconoclast Conference, and use her experience as a measure of the Conference's success as a methodology for intercultural youthwork practice.

Maia

Maia's home life is characterized by her responsibilities as a young woman in Punjabi Indian culture. She is expected to share the duties of housework with her mother. Learning to cook and to look after the home are important preparation for her arranged marriage, which will be a matter of course in a few years' time.

Maia's school life is also a large part of her social life (apart from her visits to family with family!). She is the only non-white member of her friendship group, and conversation inevitably takes place on a white agenda in terms of boys, music, fashion and so on. Most of her friends have never been to her house more than once – some never.

Maia is embarrassed about those parts of her life that are distinctively Asian when she is with her friends at school, and yet enjoys them when in conversation with other Asians or at home. She would like school better if there were more Asian people there, and enjoys going to visit her cousin in Birmingham for this reason. The presence of a larger Asian population there means that being Asian feels 'more normal, more acceptable' there. For example, Maia would not be caught dead wearing an Indian suit to the shops in Oxford, but often does so when out in Birmingham without feeling self-conscious!

Maia's family speak Punjabi at home, and attend an Asian church. They watch *Eastenders*, *The Bill* and so on as well as Indian films and the Asian cable channel. Maia likes Indian food, and can make perfect chapattis – and she loves chips!

Maia's life is one of constant negotiation between two worlds, two cultures, both of which ring true in parts. At school she feels she can't participate in conversations about going out to town, boyfriends and so on. At home she is unable to reveal her own thoughts on subjects such as men or her ambitions.

Maia found Iconoclast an emancipating experience. All that she did not feel able to talk about with her friends at school, and all that she could not express in her life at home, she found she was able to bring out in the safe space the Conference provided. Remarkably, Maia went from being one of the more reserved members of the group at school to one of the most vocal and participative at Iconoclast. The best part of the conference for Maia was being able to talk about Asian issues, her home life and her family background, with pride rather than embarrassment.

On returning to school, however, Maia reverted to her old ways of relating in her friendship group – reticent in conversations about anything Asian, and laughing at herself out of embarrassment at her Asianness before anyone else might laugh at her. Iconoclast is always something she remembers as a really good time and experience, but its lessons have made little difference to her everyday reality. The freedom of the weekend lent her courage to speak, but school meant she had to go back to a different way of relating.

The Iconoclast Conference can only be a first step towards challenging world views and changing habits of relating in everyday life. Clearly there is a need for repeated forums to challenge and opportunities for change to be effected. The Conference provides the ingredients for a methodology of intercultural youthwork that needs conscious and consistent application in a relational ministry over an extended period of time. New ways of relating, which reflect the values of another Kingdom, are not easily propagated.

Identity – the Theological Task

Another weakness of the model offered by the Iconoclast Conference lies in its understanding and exploration of a person's identity. Reference to the context of the Asian young women examined at the start of the paper may help provide some understanding here.

At present, Asian young people appear to have two options. The first may be described as 'cultural schizophrenia', where they live in two worlds according to two different mindsets and ethical frameworks. That way they never resolve who they are in order to live in integrity with their selfhood. The second is a kind of 'cultural amnesia', whereby they become so assimilated into the mindset of Western culture that they forget their own story and history. With that they never discover their 'self', their *actual*, as opposed to their *assumed*, identity.

There must be a third way, a creative identity in keeping with history and future, with inherited East and encountered West, born out of the struggle and not as anaesthetic to its pain. This third way must not be that of their parents' generation, for that would mean becoming culturally 'fossilized'. Culture evolves from generation to generation – what has meaning for, and gives meaning to, their parents' generation must change in order to be meaningful for their generation. Being true to their Asian identity cannot necessitate clinging to the static cultural form of an inherited tradition – in its 'homeland', after all, it is living and evolving all the time. This point remains true for those young people from other minority ethnic groups.

What I mean by 'actual' identity is neither inherited culture nor legal stamp or passport; nor is it an identity prescribed by those from the dominant (or another) culture. Rather, by 'actual' I mean our identity as purposed by and in God. Hence, the question of identity choices poses a theological challenge. As a model for youth ministry, a paradigm shift in focus and in methodology of practice is necessary, as exploration and discovery of this understanding must be addressed as a theological task.

This spiritual identity should make sense of our cultural identity, not destroy it. Redemption through Christ is part of the creative activity of the Trinity; salvation comes through God's gift of rebirth. St Ephrem the Syrian, in one of his hymns, describes the creative nature of Christ's redemptive activity, seen in the accounts of Jesus' miracles of healing and bringing the dead back to life:

He is the Son of the Creator
Who came to restore the whole creation.
He renewed the sky since fools worshipped
all the luminaries. He renewed the earth
that had grown old because of Adam. A new creation
came to be by his spittle, and the All-sufficient
set straight bodies and minds.

Hymns on the nativity, No. 17, v. 11–12[7]

So, if the third way for young people from minority ethnic groups is to be a redemptive one, one that brings selfhood and wholeness as opposed to either separateness or assimilation – both of which are brokenness – then the Gospel for them may be some new creative activity of God as opposed to any existing social option. As Jesus said, 'No one sews a patch of new cloth on an old garment, for the patch will pull away from the garment, making the tear worse' (Matthew 9.16 NIV).

> See, I am doing a new thing! Now it springs up; do you not perceive it?
>
> Isaiah 43.19 NIV

Yet this creative activity of God's brings about something new out of what already is – it is characterized by restoration, by transformation, by renewal and by regeneration. Perhaps, just as Christ – incarnate in history – offers the chance to be born again, what is needed here is a cultural renaissance, born out of our history, not in spite of it.

The fact of the Incarnation shows that God, though wholly 'other', does not understand Himself as separate from His creation. He acts in history and with it, He cooperates with His creation in order to transform and redeem it. He reveals Himself within our culture – we do not have to attempt the impossible: the attainment of a faith that is divorced from any culture. Our faith itself has wholeness and meaning and purpose when it becomes incarnate in our culture.

The Good News for the Asian girls may be the discovery of the third way as their spiritual identity in Christ, which, in its full sense, would also mean discovering their selfhood and, with it, their social identity in their ambiguous, multicultural world.

However, if the search for the third way is a theological task, it must be an indigenous pursuit. The journey of these young women into a faith that speaks with integrity into their lives must be one that is embarked on with *cultural* and therefore theological integrity – that is, by making sense of God from their particular cultural perspective. What is needed is a situational theology, one that speaks out of their lives and experience in order for the universal Gospel to be relevant to them. It must be an Asian-British theology that arises out of their generational and multicultural context. Similarly, other black-British theologies need to be developed in this way.

> The question arises as to whether I can truly grasp the truth of the Incarnation if I am trying to be someone else.
>
> Reverend Ronald Nathan[8]

The challenge for the Church or, more specifically, for youth ministry, is to enable these and all black young people to begin the task of theologizing – not as a hobby or activity as a consequence of a faith commitment, but as part of their journey to faith. The Christian faith that they make their own must make sense *in* their unique place of cultural tension, in order for the Gospel it embraces to make sense *of* their lives. So, wrestling with their understanding of God must somehow be addressed simultaneously with grappling with issues of culture, equality and identity – in fact, the whole gamut of concerns that impact on their understanding of self.

The Asian Christian girls at School B have much to learn from the Asian Muslim girls at School A. First, there is an important theological lesson in the Muslims' world view that sees no separation between religion and culture. Moreover, while the Muslim girls may not have resolved their struggle with their identity, they have at least retained an understanding of themselves as distinct from the dominant culture. This recognition of difference gives them strength in their struggle for selfhood as they have allowed themselves more openness with which to work out and establish their 'Asianness'. Importantly, too, this recognition of cultural difference is more in keeping with the account in Acts of the Holy Spirit's activity at Pentecost than is the effort to 'fit in' made by the

Asian Christian girls. However, the present self-understanding and identity of girls in both groups remains broken and inadequate as both involve allegiance to a culture that does not ring true to the *whole* of their self.

Cultural diversity is God-given and therefore something to be celebrated and embraced. It is the security of identity in Christ that means that positive embracing of one's own identity need not preclude celebration of another's. Moreover, it is this celebration of diversity that prevents unity in Christ from being interpreted as uniformity in Christ.

The African theologian John Mbiti describes the Gospel as coming 'to each culture as a stranger, a stranger who settles down. The Gospel does not throw out culture – instead, it settles in the culture and makes its impact on the lives of the people within that culture.[9] Perhaps there is a sense in which Asian Christians in Britain, and those from other minority ethnic groups, can use this understanding of the incarnate Gospel as a model for their own lives. The Gospel does not reject culture, but transforms it and takes it forward. Similarly the Asian's encounter with Western British culture can be a transforming impact rather than rebounding into separateness and alienation. Moreover the Gospel is not lessened or extinguished by the culture where it settles, but, rather, it speaks as a prophetic voice out of it; culture is judged by it and challenged by it. Young people from minority ethnic groups can be a prophetic voice in British society, rather than conforming beyond distinction.

For the Christian faith to be part of the process of positive social change for young people, making sense of their relationship with God must not be separated from making sense of their cultural identity. It is when they can begin to make personal and theological sense of what is truly meant by the term 'multicultural' that they can become partakers and creators of a society that uses the term with integrity, a society that embraces the richness and values of a future Kingdom. The task for youth ministry is to make it so.

CHAPTER 8

How Far is Too Far? Becoming a Woman in Church-based Youthwork

SANDRA MILLAR

Introduction

During one summer, I was involved in one of those perennial discussions that take place with younger teenage girls. It was late at night, towards the end of our two-week Christian camp, and about 12 of us were sitting around in the dark. The dark is important because it allows you to ask or say anything without fear of embarrassment. Slowly but surely the discussion moved through the usual topics – friends, dating, kissing, how far is too far? But then a new twist appeared. The question 'how far is too far?' was asked in another guise, as the young women began to wonder about their own future in the Church and society. In spite of the many changes in both the Church and society, it would seem that the future is still very unclear for girls maturing in a Christian youthwork context. This paper draws on some discussions like this, together with my research into women working with young people in the Church and women's experience of learning faith, to raise some issues about how the future looks for girls, and the implications that this might have for youthwork.

For many years, women's work has been circumscribed by their domestic role, either in practical ways or in the type of work they are assigned.[1] The myth that motherhood is the most fulfilling role a woman can have still shapes the values that women put on their own lives, as well as the value ascribed to them.[2] These values are also an integral part of women's experience of being in the Church, and that includes the experience of young girls. When a value is so fundamentally embedded, it becomes very difficult for those involved to isolate it and assess its implications objectively. The 1996 report on the Church of England youthwork, 'Youth a Part?', conspicuously ignores issues concerning gender. The identity and status of women – and girls becoming women – in the Church is bound up with gender and family issues and values in society, and, yet, for the most part, gender is not seen to affect the way in which women are able to function.[3] Within this context, Christian youthwork is failing to deliver an alternative to the models of womanhood so strongly portrayed in contemporary culture.

This paper will present a brief overview of the issues around becoming a woman in our society, and then focus on becoming a woman in the Church. It will then move on to a discussion of the tensions that exist, drawing on my research data, before a brief conclusion suggesting the implications of the research for youthwork practitioners.

Becoming a Woman In Society – Constructing Gender

Debate still continues about the extent and variety of factors that contribute towards the construction of gender behaviour in our society.[4] However, there is some agreement that gender is not just a result of nature, but is, rather, a culmination of a number of key activities and communications that create and reinforce expectations of certain types of behaviours. Through the 1970s and 1980s, seminal research from those such as Sue Sharpe (1976) and Ann Oakley (1985, also E. Figes, 1986) drew attention to educational and economic factors in defining women's roles, and the literature continues to identify and analyse gender issues across a whole range of societal structures, institutions and practices.

However, in spite of what is perceived as a global restructuring of gender roles, there is still an implicit understanding in our culture that women are responsible for childbearing and childrearing. This dichotomy or conflict of values can be identified in a variety of current structures and communications and I want to outline very briefly the current messages about women being given to girls in three key areas: school, career and media. Within the school system, there have been significant changes during this century in both the opportunities for girls in their experience of school and in the options offered to them for their future.[5] However, while care might be taken in the curriculum and language to give equality of opportunity, there is an indication that girls still struggle to engage fully in areas such as sciences, sports, physical activities and leadership. Gender stereotypes still exist, but, in some ways, girls are finding their voice and carving a place for themselves within the educational world.

As girls look ahead to the workplace, they will find a similar pattern. There has been a shift to make a place for women in a number of different areas, but the experience of many women is still of a glass ceiling, albeit raised somewhat compared to where it was a few years ago.[6] Women are still more likely to be paid less than men, to be part-time workers or to be part of the so-called flexible workforce, which can be taken in and put out of employment with ease.[7] Whereas most girls might now expect to be part of the paid workforce, their work is often still perceived as secondary, subservient to the male income and career path.

One of the most significant influences on girls, shaping their expectations of their identity and their role, is the teenage magazine culture.[8] There are other aspects of the media as well, but this is one that has been in the public arena recently. A brief look at some of the headlines, articles and adverts in a random selection of current magazines reveals one overriding message to young women: identity is found in relationships, preferably an exclusive heterosexual relationship. Looking 'right', knowing the 'right' things, having the 'right' interests are simply tools to help the young woman in her quest to find a successful partnership. Messages about opportunity and alternative roles other than partner are limited and subservient to the main idea. It is still clear that the most significant roles for women in our society are mate and, perhaps, mother, rather than economic provider and leader.[9] Becoming a woman in society is, then, a tension between the overt messages around career and opportunity, and the hidden value system that still affirms that a woman's *real* success will come through home and family. However, the message may be perceived differently for those girls growing up in a Christian culture and value system.

Becoming a Woman In the Church – Knowing Your Place

Whereas the messages in broader society are mixed for young women, the situation is simpler within the Church. An emphasis on the primary roles of mother, wife and homemaker, fits well into contemporary church life. The Church communicates that it feels comfortable with supportive, domestic, non-threatening women and that women are both weak and yet of higher spiritual purity, needing and deserving protection.[10] The Church places a particularly high priority on the role of woman as mother, partly out of a belief that women are 'instinctively' equipped for caring and nurturing,[11] specifically of young people, but also as a result of a long spiritual tradition that implies that a truly Godly woman is one who raises children in obedience to God and parents, is both a pious mother and an obedient wife.[12] More recently, churches have absorbed the Bowlby theories of maternal deprivation,[13] so women who work outside the home are often prey to particular guilt and pressure within the Church. These ideas are by no means limited to the traditional churches. Some of the fast-growing new churches, which may appear radically different in many ways, hold the most rigid and conservative views about the roles of women.[14]

The language the Church uses to describe and define both itself and its members, and also to perform its task, is often limiting in the way it portrays women. Girls learn from an early age of that strange linguistic trick whereby the male pronoun also includes them and the Church. Church-linked organizations, including youth and children's work, still use this in much of their language.[15]

Another powerful means by which values and expectations are transmitted is via metaphor. Metaphors bring understanding to complicated situations, but are also used to describe and define pre-existing institutions and organizations. One of the most common metaphors that the Church uses to describe itself is that of the family, and this carries significant implications for gender roles within the organizational structure.

The family metaphor contributes to the definition of authority and spheres of influence within the Church's organizational structure, where men are found in leadership, public office and finance, while women are involved with children and hospitality. The metaphor can also constrain creativity and initiative, particularly for women and young people, encouraging passivity and dependence, therefore simply maintaining the established order for the sake of social and economic stability rather than offering any radical alternative model for our society.

The family metaphor also carries with it implications about power and where power lies.[16] Within a patriarchal family structure, power is clearly with the male, especially the father, and again this is reflected in the Church.[17] A male-dominated organizational culture presents particular difficulties for those seeking to bring about changes in these values, and, in some situations, including the Church, women have had to play the male role and adopt male-type behaviour in order to have influence and power.

For girls observing and learning about their potential within the Church, there is a clear message. The Church simply echoes the message of the magazines by saying that real fulfilment comes via the roles of partnering a male and bringing up children. It does not have the problem of trying to help women balance or juggle a multiplicity of roles because it implicitly undervalues other roles. Much of the discussion of women's roles in the Church has concentrated on issues concerning leadership and ordination, but there are a vast number of women who do not seek leadership and yet their lives and faith are being limited by the gender expectations and values that are both explicitly and implicitly communicated in their chosen Christian context. Drawing on data collected from participant discussions and interviews, I will now consider more specifically the implications of the gender practices for youthwork.

Girls, Women and the Future

Girls in Doubt

As has already been indicated, girls draw their information from a number of sources as they learn how they will fulfil their adult role in society. These include school, home, media and friends,[18] and for girls who are part of a Christian culture, this will also include the Church and the youthwork.

My research indicates that almost all of those working with children under the age of 10 are women, and that this proportion decreases as the age range increases, so that men are the predominant leaders with those 14 and over, although women may be actively involved in support roles. Recent observations of this tendency include the Brainstormers event, where attendance was approximately 65 per cent male, and the Church of England Day Conference for full-time youth workers, where over 80 per cent of attendees were male (both occurred in 1996). These events are a reflection of the situation in other youthwork, and also in broader occupational fields, such as teaching, nursing and library services. There will be an impact on young people of seeing that children are taught almost entirely by women and that leadership is exclusively male.[19]

Alongside the visible modelling of gender relationships, there is also the implication of the hidden curriculum whereby values are communicated via the teaching and messages that are given. For example, teaching on God as Father often stereotypes fathers as busy, distant and preoccupied, but ignores the impact that mothers might have in forming a young person's perception of God, and also stereotypes both men and women into certain roles, behaviour and expectations. Young people are working with a very male-dominated construct of God and the Church and this is not helpful to their ability to redefine the quality of life for either males or females within the Church.[20] In discussions about their future, girls express quite serious worries abut the potential roles for women in the Church. The participant discussions revealed a great deal of ambivalence about the power and influence that they might have in the future. Phrases such as 'having a say' or 'supporting my husband' and 'behind the scenes' cropped up as the girls struggled to express what they think their future role might be. They expressed conservative and traditional views about giving up work to look after children, and children and husbands coming first. They discussed the idea of women in leadership, echoing the arguments that have come from their spokespeople, several of them finding it strange to have a woman involved in leading worship or teaching. Some of them were touchingly anxious about whether or not it is right to want to be a leader as they struggled with their own undoubted potential and desire to belong in the Christian and Church culture.

On another occasion they were asked to name a famous person in each of 30 major categories of public life, from sport to music to politics. The maximum number of women named by any girl was four and they included a film star, a singer and Mother Teresa; none of them could name a woman church leader. The world of Christian young women is peopled with male role models, indicating a world of limited opportunities and confirming their expectations that their identity as women is tied up with their ability to make relationships – hence, both the Christian and secular preoccupation in youth communication with sex and dating. Asked about singleness and childlessness, all of the girls seemed unable to face this as a concept, except as a kind of second best that they would battle to come to terms with as a positive experience for them. Girls are doubtful about their future in the Church and, later, I will return to this and suggest what the possible implications are.

Women in Faith

My current research is concerned with how women experience their personal faith within the framework of the Church's organization. The primary means of expressing faith is in terms of task and activity, and personal faith is also intrinsically related to their roles within the organization. 'Before I was involved with the Church . . . the Church then became an extension of my involvement with the Lord – serving the Church would be a way of serving Him . . .' Nearly always, current learning and faith development is expressed in terms of activity, problem-solving and current situations. This might refer to difficulties in the youth group leadership or the Church's management, but whatever the particular activity, it is clearly something that gives identity and value both personally and within the wider community. Faith, then, becomes related to the public, external world of concrete reason, which is more acceptable and communicable than an internal, relational, intuitive activity. Hence women's faith only becomes visible and acceptable when it is translated into the public, and male, world.[21]

As has already been discussed, the Church, like many organizations, reflects the gender values of the culture in which we live, which, even now, expect women to be in the domestic world and men in the public sphere. This, in turn, has power implications in the relationship between the private domestic world of women and the external, wage-earning world of men. Extending this from the home into the organization, women may have expertise and skill, but men have authority, so, in terms of personal faith, women need to validate their experience by taking it into the external world. However, it still remains domestic rather than authoritative. This desire to be involved fully in the external world of task and activity may also indicate the tension that exists between the stated desire to fulfil a primary role as mother and homemaker and a need to be using skills and abilities in a wider sphere. As women increase their educational attainments and achieve greater status in the workplace, the differences between this and their role and experience in the Church will be accentuated. While they may outwardly agree that their place is in the home, they are also actively pursuing other visible, voluntary roles. However, volunteer work rarely brings authority and power, although it may involve a presence in the external public world.[22]

Much of the imagery used in talking about faith is concerned with ladders or journeys that lead to predetermined goals. There is a certainty about direction and truth, and this type of learning – determinedly pursuing 'the right answer' – typifies male hierarchical models of knowledge acquisition. There is a strong need to conform and to participate in the big picture of church life on the right terms. The struggle to conform might be likened to the induction process in any large company, where the new employee has to learn both the explicit and implicit culture of the organization and, often, those who do not fit the normative expectations – women, disabled, black, aged – struggle to find their place.[23] This inculturation process also takes place in the Church and girls are learning that, to enter and be accepted in the faith community, they need to conform to certain expectations – being a supporter, a mother, a volunteer, and pursue faith and truth on a preordained journey.[24]

However, my research indicates that the development and learning of faith may not be such a linear, external process for women. As C. Gilligan suggested in her study on moral reasoning and women, women are more unstructured and relational in the ways in which they explore abstract dilemmas and issues than men.[25] So, girls need space to question, explore and build a wide range of inclusive relationships as they learn to belong in the faith community. They need to see and know women who are at ease with themselves and their faith, and who are able to help them to process their faith and doubt in ways that allow girls to develop as women before God.

Youthwork in Tension

As has already been observed, the particular understanding of family within the Church is largely a conservative, patriarchal model, reflecting the idealized picture of family life that emerged at the end of the last century.[26] This view that women will be most fulfilled as wives, and especially as mothers, is also a central feature of church life and one that resonates surprisingly easily with the mainstream of society. This understanding becomes outwardly visible in the roles and duties that are considered acceptable for women within the Church. One of the major responsibilities of women is the nurture and education of young people and, in addition, women become responsible for domestic and support roles and also are visible in the caring aspects of church life, such as hospital visiting and working with the elderly.[27]

The structure and place of young people's work within the overall organizational structure does itself give rise to certain tensions and expectations for the girls it seeks to serve. Women who are themselves involved in this work have an awareness of the low esteem in which they are frequently held. 'I think they felt that, one, who were we, we hadn't any training, we were just a group of mothers, we may not be reliable, it may be a flash in the pan, and after a few minutes we may finish. Um, yeah, I don't think they thought we were capable, basically.' If those women who are involved in being role models for girls are themselves caught up in the tension between duties and responsibilities and yet limited in power and influence, then they are themselves unable to give positive alternative messages to the values being communicated through the media and reinforced in the Church. Women are often aware of the need to see fundamental changes in the way young people's work is structured, arguing that while children are seen as the sole prerogative of women, then the status of women will also remain low. This argument has also been put forward on a wider platform,[28] suggesting that society needs to reassess radically its perception of where responsibility for child and youth nurture lies.

However, the experience of trying to bring about change is not an easy one and the women talked about trying to make an impact within the Church and the sense of conflict and isolation that followed. 'A lot of people I spoke to all said the same thing – we're fighting with our churches, it's a losing battle, nobody wants to listen to us, nobody wants to hear us, and it was the same thing time in and time out.' Women in a range of organizations identify difficulty in trying to bring about change and translate their ideas into reality. This lack of real authority and frustration with the structure is another consequence of a patriarchal church structure, where women and youth are less important than men. This is then reflected in the conscious or unconscious practices and actions towards these groups of people and, together with the perceptions of motherhood and the voluntary nature of the task, means that female youth and children's workers are marginalized within the Church.

The women I interviewed who work with young people revealed a group who are committed and caring, yet who also have a deep sense of being unappreciated by the rest of the organization. This is a corollary of the patterns found in family life and also the workplace, where women are limited by the expectations placed on them by themselves and others. The long-term effect of constantly feeling insignificant was summed up by one of the interviewees:

> I think that's what's happened to women in the Church, too. For so long they've been told that things aren't important or you

> don't need to bring that up now or pass that on to one of the others, but in fact when they do have ideas or visions or whatever, they just sit on them and they die because they just can't be bothered to go through the hassle.

Given the tensions inherent in this statement, it becomes very difficult for girls to answer the question 'how far is too far?' in terms of their leadership and potential roles within the Christian faith community. It would seem that those who work with them have recognized the difficulty of trying to change, and that there is a deep-seated pressure for women to remain with the children and find fulfilment in supportive roles, echoes of the teenage magazine.

Conclusion – Turning the Tide

For young girls growing up in a Christian environment, the Church is one of the places that will reinforce or challenge the values that are communicated through home, school and the media. Young people learn about the issues that are important, about relationships, conflict, values and judgement by listening, watching and participating in the world of adults, and one of the core values that is being learnt is the way that men and women interact in our society. Messages about the value of women, and assumptions about their tasks and roles, are being formed during adolescence – a key time for establishing gender identity and sex roles. The primary message still remains one that support roles are both desirable and valuable for women.

On the one hand, the Church reinforces the idea that value is found primarily in exclusive partnering relationships and, on the other, it offers few opportunities for leadership and real authority to those who want to pursue alternative goals. Alternatives are being given to girls in school and the workplace. They no longer simply want to be in support roles; they believe they can be opinion formers, not just followers. Yet, the Church does not offer them that. So, young girls are either forced to live out yet another kind of dualism – performing the role of submissive, obedient girl in the Church while forging ahead in school – or are reassured that finding a boyfriend is the primary goal, acceptable both in the

Church and society. Alternatively, she leaves the Church because the Christian community has nothing to offer her in answer to her questions.

My research is concerned with making a difference in the lives of women as they experience Christianity. As both a researcher and a practitioner in youthwork, a paper such as this is frustrating to those of us who want to turn the tide – it raises issues and questions, but puts forward no easy solutions. Further questions need to be asked, and new models of youthwork developed and researched. Opportunities for girls to develop leadership, together with healthy role models and attention to language and stereotyping, may well be needed if the Church is to offer a radical alternative for young women. By raising awareness of the extent to which girls are overlooked, marginalized and limited by the Church and its youth programmes, I hope that more questions will be asked and evaluation and change set in motion. And maybe one day the honest answer that we will be able to give to the question, 'how far is too far?' will be, 'as far as your God-given dreams and abilities will take you', regardless of gender and society.

CHAPTER 9

Roots and Wings: Practising Theology with Youth

DON C. RICHTER

Rhythms of Faith

It's Sunday evening. Senior high youth gather in their designated room for a weekly youth fellowship meeting. This is a large, United Methodist congregation in suburban Chicago. It can afford to pay a seminary student to run its youth programme. Susan, the seminarian, announces that tonight's programme is about 'rhythms of faith'. She begins by asking the group to identify different kinds of rhythms in nature, such as the changing of the seasons. Susan lists their responses on newsprint.

Present this evening are 18 youth and four adults. Julie, a 16-year-old high school junior, leans over and whispers something to her friend Beth. Susan notices Julie whispering and Beth nodding in agreement. 'Julie, why don't you share your thoughts with the rest of the group.' Julie blushes silently, but Susan persists: 'Now if it's worth saying, it's worth saying to the whole group.'

Julie glances fleetingly at Beth, then looks at the floor and says in a halting voice, 'Well, I was just thinking about my body's monthly rhythm, you know, my period, and wondering how that relates to what we're talking about . . .'

'Oh man!' explodes Robert, the group clown. He and his side-kicks begin snickering and poking at one another. Some of the younger girls in the group laugh nervously.

'That's enough, guys', Susan says sharply, trying to call the meeting back to order. 'Julie, I don't think this is an appropriate topic for our discussion tonight. We'll talk about it some other time.' Julie, still looking at the floor, nods her head and ponders how to deal with the embarrassment she feels. The programme continues as Susan asks the group to think about whether the life of faith has any particular rhythms or seasons.

The above incident was witnessed by a seminarian who observed this youth group meeting as part of an assignment for a course I taught in youth ministry. Students were asked to identify the explicit, implicit, and null curricula in an educational event involving youth.[1] The encounter between Susan and Julie is a powerful illustration of how explicit curriculum is modified by null curriculum – that is, what's taught in a lesson is shaped by what's left out, omitted, silenced. The youth group was taught that the female body is not a proper subject for theological reflection. Ironically, this lesson was taught by a female seminarian, a woman training for ministry in the United Methodist Church.

We could chronicle the long patriarchal history of the Church that results in one woman conveying an oppressive, sexist ideology to other women, or we could examine the dynamics of disgust and revulsion that adolescent males express towards the female body.[2] What I want to do in this essay, however, is to present a constructive alternative to this story. I want to describe a programme called the Youth Theology Institute that I helped launch at Emory University in Atlanta, Georgia, in 1992. YTI, as we call it, sponsors a four-week, ecumenical summer academy for 60 rising high school seniors from across the USA. YTI is for teenagers like Julie who are posing fundamental questions regarding faith and everyday life. YTI is also for youth leaders like Susan who need different models for faithful ministry with young people.

A primary impetus for establishing YTI has been the need to reconceive the way youth are viewed within society and within the Church. We'll begin with a brief review of the social construct of adolescence, then we'll identify ways in which the Church has responded to contemporary perceptions of youth and youth culture. Finally, I will describe the mission and goals of the YTI. I will underscore what we are learning about youth through our research, and advocate that similar programmes be undertaken in every country represented at this conference. The value of YTI, I submit, is not in its novelty or uniqueness, but, rather, in its paradigmatic quality as a youth movement for our day and time. There are Julies everywhere who yearn for a safe place to wonder, for a ministry that will give them roots in a tradition as well as wings to explore new ideas and practices.

The Social Construct of Adolescence

Let us first review the social construct of contemporary adolescence. The evidence is now clear and compelling: our current view of teenagers as 'adolescents' is a recent cultural invention. In Europe and North America, the notion of 'adolescence' as an extension of 'pubescence' is a social by-product of twentieth-century industrialization. Simply put, youth and youth culture were invented because we needed them. With the shift from manual labour to machines, and the emergence of a professional class requiring prolonged education, a new stage of life was defined for teenagers. Instead of learning a trade, running the farm or working in a factory, teenagers were expected – no, required – to go to school. Instead of getting married and having children, teenagers were encouraged to abstain from or practise 'safe' sex.[3]

As the conception of what teenagers are to be and do has shifted, the religious concept of 'vocation' has been replaced by psychological and cultural concepts of vocation. Theologically, vocation is dialogical and relational: a voice (God) calls and another party (a human being) responds to that voice. Vocation has as much to do with who I am and who I am becoming as it does with what I choose to do in terms of career, work, job or occupation. From a Christian perspective, vocation 'is the response a person makes with his or her total self to the address of God and to the calling to partnership.'[4] Theologically, we claim that everyone has a God-given vocation at every stage of life.

The shift towards a psychological vocation for adolescence is rooted in G. Stanley Hall's seminal essay of 1904 defining this stage of life as a period of *Sturm und Drang*. What makes this such a stormy, tumultuous period is more than raging hormones; it is coping with the requirements of modern society. Premodern societies were characterized by relatively static social roles determined by family of origin, race, class and gender. A person's religious background, for instance, was a social given. Modern societies are characterized by a high degree of structural differentiation, requiring individuals to negotiate a variety of social roles on an everyday basis. Not only are individuals now free to choose, but they are obligated to choose from a range of roles. Peter Berger describes this shift from fate to choice as 'the heretical imperative'. Once, heretics were persecuted, but now everyone is required to be a heretic, to choose one's own spiritual path in the world.[5]

For teenagers today, personal identity is no longer a given; it is a developmental achievement. E. Erikson defines the task as that of constructing a coherent identity in the face of role confusion.[6] Youth are encouraged to embark on a journey of self-discovery, to 'find themselves' or, less tactfully, to 'get a life'. Everyday life requires individuals to manage a variety of social roles. Youth must learn the appropriate rules and roles governing a particular context and they must learn to distance themselves from the roles they adopt in each sphere. In becoming adults, youth must learn to 'play' different roles without identifying themselves fully with any one of them.[7]

Closely connected with this psychological vocation is a cultural vocation for youth. From childhood on, young people are taught to listen, watch, and consume rather than to speak, envision, and act. In advanced market economies, persons are valued not for their potential to produce, but for their potential to consume. The so-called 'youth culture' is a prime example of an adult-generated, financially motivated marketing strategy. Teenagers do not create youth culture, nor do they inherit it by virtue of their chronological status. Teenagers consume youth culture by purchasing their way into it. Youth culture is a commodity to be bought and sold.[8]

The marketing of youth culture has led to the marketing of youth themselves. In the last decade of the twentieth century, young people are perceived more as a financial liability than an asset. Children and teenagers who internalize this cultural message will come to believe that their value lies less in what they are than in what they have achieved. There is no concept of ascriptive worth here. Young people learn to market themselves in order to convince others – and themselves, and perhaps God – that they are worth while and have value. Youth are encouraged to view the work of adolescence as chalking up more and more experiences on their resumés, regardless of whether or not these experiences have ever been interpreted and integrated into their lives. Cv now stands for 'cosmic vitae' as much as for 'curriculum vitae'. Marketing oneself to the cosmos has become an ontological enterprise for youth.

Youth have a psychological vocation to choose and construct their identity. They have a cultural vocation to market themselves. Few teenagers have a sense of religious vocation, however, unless they understand the term as denoting entry into a religious order. Only the sanctified life of the religious professional counts as a bona fide vocation – everyone else just works for a living. As we recall, Martin Luther launched a Reformation against the notion that the life of faith was the exclusive purlieu of cloistered monks. Luther, and reformers after him, redefined Christian vocation as the specific call to love our neighbour in the midst of life's ordinary, day-to-day activities. As we pray each morning for our daily bread, Luther observed, people are already busy at work in the bakeries.[9]

How has the Church responded in this century to the social construct of adolescence? In what ways has the Church co-opted the prevailing view of youth and youth culture? In what ways has the Church challenged the shift towards psychological and cultural vocations for adolescence? In the section below, I will briefly describe three modes of response: protection, self-actualization and tribal initiation.

Responses of the Church to 'Adolescence'

Protection

During the nineteenth century, the Sunday school movement had already identified 'youth' as a discrete stage of life that required its own age-graded, age-segregated curriculum. The emerging psychology movement reinforced such sponsored, adult-led activities and programmes. Religious communities accommodated their ministry to this youth group model, and 'youth fellowship groups' were organized at local, regional, and national levels.

Currently, conventional approaches to ministry with youth immerse teenagers in some form of adult-sponsored youth group. North American youth viewed as 'high school students' are inducted into the local church youth group when they begin the seventh or ninth grade, and are 'graduated' from the programme when they complete high school. The youth group model provides a holding environment for young adolescents. Activities rarely focus on the social practices and occupations of the adult world. It is therefore not uncommon for high school juniors and seniors to drop out of their youth group and cease participating in congregational life altogether.

The youth group model is historically rooted in the desire to protect teenagers. The virtue of this model is that youth do indeed need safe places to gather for fellowship. At its best, the youth group is a launching pad for service learning and outreach. The danger of the youth group model is in defining the interests, attitudes and desires of youth in terms of their own age cohort. Protection can become domestication when the implicit curriculum admonishes youth to play it safe and stay out of trouble. Youth are then taught to navigate between narrow, socially acceptable boundaries, avoiding destructive impulses on one side and any summons to heroic action on the other.[10] The domestication mode accepts current conceptions of youth and youth culture uncritically. Such forms of ministry do not provide youth with either roots or wings.

Self-actualization

The Church's second mode of response to youth culture has been to promote self-actualization. According to this view, youth need to be 'liberated' from conventional religion in order to form their own world view. This approach emphasizes the private spiritual quest and advises young people to take a break from institutional religion, to distance themselves from tradition today in order to reclaim it tomorrow. A self-actualization approach draws heavily on theories of adolescent development, including the need of youth to differentiate themselves from social roles. The implicit message of many confirmation programmes is that, once confirmed, youth are free to follow their own spiritual trajectories for a while. This is especially true for older teens, who often leave home with no plans for corporate worship during their college years. We trust that youth who have drifted away from the Church will somehow return to the fold when they get married and have children themselves.

Tribal initiation

The self-actualization mode of response has been popular in liberal Protestantism, where adults themselves are switching traditions or dropping out in record numbers. The pendulum has swung so far in the other direction, suggests Duke University Chaplain Will Willimon, that the way college students scandalize parents today is to return home at semester break and announce that they have become a Christian – not an atheist, which would have scandalized parents in previous generations.

Willimon and his colleague Stanley Hauerwas argue passionately that what youth need today are religious roots, not the wings of Enlightenment liberalism. They contend that it is misguided for the Church to tell youth to 'think for themselves', for when we do this, we are simply abandoning young people to think with the aid of dominant cultural images supplied by consumer capitalism. We cannot truly liberate youth, claim Willimon and Hauerwas, unless we initiate them into a tribe that confesses and practises the Christian Story. The task of the Church is to form people into 'resident aliens', not socially well-adapted consumers.[11]

In some ways, the tribal initiation mode resembles the protection mode of response: we must protect our young people from the hostile world out there; we must choose for them rather than asking them to choose for themselves. The chief difference, however, is that tribal initiation is a function of the local faith community, not a response to psychological or cultural definitions of adolescence. Tribal initiation depends on learner readiness – regardless of age – and is not merely an accommodation to cultural demands for a puberty rite. The local congregation is called to take responsibility for the ongoing spiritual formation of its members throughout their lives. Forming teenagers as Christians requires an extended, challenging, high-expectations initiation process. Only then will youth be genuinely protected and liberated.

The tribal initiation mode enables a recovery of the concept of religious vocation for youth. Youth can be who God calls them to be not by defining themselves in terms of youth culture or youth groups or youth activities, but by defining themselves as human beings who are summoned and drawn to particular commitments in life. Karl Barth offers instructive counsel in this regard:

> We can be young only when we are moved by something which in itself has nothing at all to do with youth or age, and in relation to which we are summoned and drawn even as young people. We can be young only in specific demonstration of our preparedness, attention, zeal, and obedience, only in youthful objectivity, not by chasing the phantom of what is supposed to be 'youthful'. He who wants to be a child is not a child; he is merely childish. She who is a child does not want to be a child: she takes her play, her study, her first wrestlings with her environment in absolute earnest, as though she were already an adult. In doing so, she is genuinely childlike.[12]

The virtue of the tribal initiation mode is that it portrays the life of faith in relation to a particular set of ecclesial practices, such as prayer, Scripture reading, testimony, hymn singing and hospitality to strangers. 'Christian practices are things Christians do together over time in response to and in the light of God's active presence for the life of the world.'[13] Via participation in these practices, our moral imagination and our daily activity are shaped in powerful, fundamental ways. When the Church does not teach these Christian practices well, parents will seek moral formation for their children in other social practices, such as sports or the performing arts. In the USA, one could argue the case that parents now rely on sports to provide the kind of character formation that the Sunday school movement provided a century ago.

All of us yearn to be members of a tribe that will give us roots. Given the fragility of relational bonds, the inability of relationships to sustain conflict without collapsing, we are naturally attracted to networks of belonging that give us an identity in this complicated society. Most of us belong to several tribes, including e-mail networks with people we have never met face to face. The problem is not tribal identities, but the trap of tribalism. Tribalism obscures commitment to the common good that reaches beyond tribe. Tribalism tempts me to take care of me and mine first, and perhaps immediate others, and then make a dignified retreat into some fortified enclave defined by profession, lifestyle, ethnicity, age, class or religion.[14]

Recent research indicates that 'those who best practise a commitment to an inclusive common good are paradoxically those who can simultaneously reach across tribes and remain firmly rooted in the particularities of their own.'[15] What has enabled people to live extraordinary lives of commitment on behalf of the common good, what has enabled them to think globally and act locally over the long haul is 'constructive engagement with otherness'.[16] Constructive engagement with those who are different means moving beyond superficial encounters that reinforce stereotypes. Such engagement is important at every stage of life, but it is especially salient for teenagers as they identify themselves with particular tribes.

How can we envision a youth ministry that initiates teenagers into Christian practices while providing them with opportunities for constructive engagement with otherness? How can we simultaneously cultivate roots and unfold wings? This brings us to a description of the mission and goals of the YTI.

The Mission and Goals of the YTI

The primary mission of the YTI at Emory University is to provide an innovative programme of Christian theological education for 17-year-olds in order to cultivate a cadre of public theologians for the Church and for society. By means of an application process, every youth who is admitted to this programme is awarded a full scholarship for tuition, room and board.[17] The ultimate aim of YTI is for youth participants to fall in love with God and God's creation. A proximate aim is for YTI scholars to fall in love with theology as an ongoing practice and life-long pursuit.

'Falling in love with theology' may strike some as an odd expression. What's to love about the discipline of theology? The notion of romance is derived from Alfred North Whitehead's description of 'The rhythm of education' as the movement from romance to precision to generalization. The romance stage initiates the learning process by engaging a person's attention and passion in a particular subject matter. This stage is often characterized by excitement, adventure, and playfulness as the learner becomes aware of a new world waiting to be explored. The precision required for map-making can be temporarily suspended until the learner is ready to take the next step.[18]

The 'scholars' who participate in the YTI summer academy are perceived as young theologians, capable of relating biblical and theological texts to contemporary social activities and contexts. Towards that end, YTI is organized around six foundational curricular aims.

1 Youth join adult participants in shaping and being accountable to a residential covenant community. As a theological academy for teenagers, YTI is not encumbered by concerns for denominational survival or guild respectability. We are free to create a holistic learning environment so that scholars and staff together practise theology for everyday life. Parker Palmer's *The Company of Strangers* (Crossroad, New York, 1981) provides a framework for understanding ourselves as residential companions who must learn to cooperate as a household while respecting the particularity and even the strangeness of one another. Over a four-week period, participants have multiple opportunities to practise forgiveness as they seek to remain in covenant and hold one another accountable for commitments.

The virtue of a residential learning environment is that participants discover new ways to create life together, drawing on gifts and capacities they may not have realized they had. The emphasis is on creating a shared culture, not on consuming a pre-fabricated culture. For example, if scholars want a YTI T-shirt for their particular group, they must organize themselves to design it. If they want an audiotape of their favourite YTI songs, they need to schedule a taping session. We would do these young people a disservice if we simply offered them a menu of good experiences to consume. Scholars find that they delight much more in their own live entertainment than in passively watching television or videos.

2 Youth learn how to engage, analyse and address public issues from a Christian theological perspective. We noted above that youth have been effectively silenced as political agents in the shaping of their lives and learning. At YTI, *The Company of Strangers* lays a foundation for our examination of 'public life' and the 'common good'. Reclaiming a constructive understanding of 'public' is crucial during this period of political retreat from investment in our commonwealth. Youth who feel called to serve the public good are given opportunities to experience congregations and agencies that faithfully practise hospitality to strangers and thereby put themselves at risk for the sake of God's promises and blessings.

During the 1994 summer academy, we experienced extensive flooding throughout the state of Georgia. While the Emory campus sustained only minor water damage, communities such as Americus were devastated by overflowing rivers. The YTI community decided to postpone the planned programme in order to brainstorm faithful modes of response to this crisis. Scholars identified and carried out three related strategies. First, they volunteered with relief agencies such as the Red Cross that were already providing assistance. Second, they organized a trip to Americus and worked with Habitat for Humanity to lay sods of earth on flooded property. Third, they planned and conducted a public worship service for flood victims called 'Soaking Up the Waters', preaching on the Genesis flood story in which God remembered Noah. Via these efforts, YTI scholars learned how to become a community of moral courage and care for others.

3 Youth are guided in exploring quality theological literature, including classics of the Christian faith tradition. Teenagers need access to the vast resources of theology, both ancient and modern. Too often youth are handed watered-down reading materials – if they are handed anything at all to read. In metropolitan areas, and even in rural communities, youth have multiple

daily encounters with followers of other world religions. Christian youth find themselves ill-equipped to engage in interfaith conversations and unfamiliar with basic themes and perspectives that are present in the literature of the Christian faith tradition.

Assisted by competent adult guides, motivated 17-year-olds gather in exploratory groups to read and discuss books by theologians such as Paul Tillich, Jurgen Moltmann, Sallie McFague, Walter Wink and Ignatius Loyola. A key curricular principle is that the texts selected must have personal power and significance for the teachers. What scholars see modelled is a conversation between teacher and texts. As they come to trust their teacher, scholars are drawn into this conversation with the assigned texts as well.

4 Youth learn specific skills for how to read and interpret the Bible. The Bible is the book most teenagers have readily available for theological reflection. Unless they are involved in a formal Bible study programme (such as Disciple), youth are unlikely to have more than a devotional acquaintance with biblical literature. During YTI, scholars take a plenary course, 'Reading the Bible'. The goal of this course is to equip youth with basic skills for reading and interpreting the Bible responsibly by becoming attuned to the rhetorical style of different literary genres, examining how the Bible functions authoritatively as Scripture for different communities and identifying and examining personal biblical canons.

5 Youth experience a variety of ways to worship together as an ecumenical group, including worship with local Christian congregations and other religious communities. Young people long for the presence of God in their lives. Even as they become sophisticated and doubtful, 17-year-olds are eager to express their spiritual hunger and their heart's deep desire in private and corporate worship. Each weekend, scholars make 'pilgrimages' to worship with local faith communities. These 'constructive engagements with otherness' invite youth to reflect on rituals and forms of worship that seem strange and uncomfortable to them. In an era when Christian denominations are in a retrievalist mode, YTI practises alternative ways of mediating ecclesial reality for the sake of the future. The contributions of various

denominations are noted, and their respective practices are celebrated even as they are being relativized.[19] A guiding theological assumption is that new incarnations of the Church are coming into being, and that these new ecclesial forms are related to, yet not derivative of, those denominations that have characterized the present religious landscape.

6 Youth are affirmed in asking tough theological questions within the Church – that is, without having to leave the Church to do so. YTI provides an opportunity for youth to discover Christian theology as a resource for addressing all their questions, even ones they consider scandalous or taboo. YTI stands with youth as a community of faith that is willing to wonder with youth about their deepest questions and to struggle with them in seeking answers. It is not uncommon for scholars to leave YTI with more questions than they came with, and this ability to ask more probing and profound questions is usually acknowledged as a blessing.

Exploratory courses are one structured context for asking questions in relation to specific course content. Covenant groups provide scholars with subliminal space to discover and reflect on their own personal emergent questions. The purpose of the covenant groups is to mediate between structured classroom discussion and informal dorm conversation.

A third context for deep questioning is the personal interview. During each YTI, we use a modified form of James Fowler's 'faith development interview' protocol to conduct personal interviews with a select group of scholars. What is intriguing to our research team is the way scholars make catechetical use of these interviews to reach beyond their taken-for-granted ideas and ways of knowing. In the context of private, structured conversation with an attentive listener, scholars initially articulate their grasp of 'correct doctrine', then tender emergent concepts and thought experiments that may contradict their original doctrinal position. This productive form of speech, in which scholars sometimes 'say more than they can know' (Julia Kristeva), indicates that teenagers trust the interview as a safe space for pondering existential questions.

What YTI seems to offer female scholars, especially, is a safe place to voice these nascent concerns, to speak about the dissonance they feel, but may not have expressed openly before. Our female alumni, in commenting on the significance of YTI for their lives, have consistently underscored the self-esteem they gained from this experience. What is this quality of self-esteem that empowers these young women, and how does it relate to their spiritual life?

YTI: Research Findings

In *Women's Ways of Knowing*, Mary Belenky and her associates contend that teenage females have a more difficult time claiming the authority of their inner voice. Even economically advantaged young women tend to demur by saying 'It's just my opinion' instead of asserting 'I have a right to my opinion.' The 'good girl' approaches subjective knowing cautiously, feeling at times overwhelmed with options and fearful of ultimately being alone in her choices. She becomes a polite listener, a spectator who watches and listens but does not act. When she goes to college, she mutes her subjective voice for the sake of procedural knowing, acquiring the skills to compare and contrast in academic courses.[20]

Based on four years' experience, I submit that YTI enables female scholars to 'go public' as subjective knowers, to enter into solidarity with other females who are also finding the freedom to claim their inner voices. Whereas male alumni reflect on YTI as an experience of gaining new perspectives and new ways of thinking, female alumni often describe both a loss and a gain:

> When I got myself into YTI, I found that I was 'losing my faith', and I was completely chaotic and all these things were going through my mind and I didn't know who I was or what I believed. That went on for a long time after YTI ended. We've stayed close as friends, but I really didn't find myself faithful – not faithful but . . . I don't really know how to explain it . . . I just wasn't very religious. I didn't want to go to church and all the old things I had believed I questioned. I didn't know what I was getting myself into. It's just been in the last few months that my faith has started to build back up again. And I think I found that experience of losing my faith and regaining it has made me

> grow as a person and as a Christian and it's strengthened my relationship with Christ and with God. And without having lost that, I couldn't be the Christian that I am, I wouldn't have the relationship with Christ I have now. That's really turned my life around, and it happened because of YTI, because of what I experienced last summer. 'Mary', 1993

Mary entered YTI as an all-American 'good girl': a leader in her school and church, chair of the Presbytery youth council, strong family ties. What happened for Mary, and for other female scholars at YTI, was the objectification of the self and of faith. By means of this four-week immersion experience, and the subsequent reintegration process, Mary moved from 'being' her identity to 'having' an identity, from 'being' her faith to 'having' a faith. What was tacitly, subjectively fused with Mary (her meaning-making structure) became the object of her reflection (meaning-making content). As Robert Kegan maintains, this subject-object shift is experienced as both a loss of self and a gaining of self.[21] Cognitively, what is at stake for Mary is an emergent capacity to combine subjective knowing with both connected and separate forms of procedural knowing. Because Mary now trusts her subjective voice, she will be able to integrate this with a hermeneutics of suspicion as well as with a hermeneutics of generosity during her college years and beyond.

For 17-year-olds to risk their self-constructions during YTI, the programme must function as an adequate 'holding environment' for participants. According to Robert Kegan, a healthy holding environment provides individuals with an optimal balance of three dynamics: holding on (confirmation), letting go (contradiction) and remaining in place (continuity). We evolve as selves from a succession of 'cultures of embeddedness', and each evolution is indelibly shaped by the way we are held and let go of, and by the way we are assisted as we reintegrate our selves into a new context for personal growth.[22]

As a holding environment, YTI functions in a peculiar way in relation to a traditional church camp or conference. Typically, youth attend these latter events in the company of trusted adults they already know. A church camp or conference usually includes 'veterans', youth who have previously experienced a similar programme in this same location. Familiarity with the persons and routines serves the confirmation and continuity functions of church camp/conference holding environments.

With YTI, scholars arrive into a 'company of strangers' with no familiar adult sponsor or adviser. The potential for the holding environment dynamic or 'contradiction' is maximized for scholars. While local scholars may visit with family on Saturdays, most scholars experience little 'continuity' until they return home after YTI. When crises occur, and matters of communal discipline are called into question, staff members are sometimes polarized over how to handle the situation. We are still learning how to appeal to scholars' need for appropriate limits and boundaries as well as to their desire for responsible independence. We are practising ways to 'hold on' well to scholars and manifest non-anxious presence during their periods of crisis and emergence.

As indicated above, YTI does a good job of encouraging youth to raise new questions and to challenge previous world views. We are heartened when we hear our alumni describe how they have been empowered by YTI:

> In English literature you read about 'the Wanderer', and I identify with that character, 'the Wanderer'. I'm continuously searching, searching . . . and I was not 'the Wanderer' until I came to YTI. And when I left, I became that Wanderer. I continue searching and searching, trying to find the answers to my life and trying to find some possible solutions to our world's problems. That is why I'm determined, after I graduate from Georgetown, to return to Mississippi to try to solve a lot of the problems of my home state. 'Jared', 1993

We are also aware that we have little control over how YTI scholars are reintegrated back into their home communities. For some, the return home is a greater culture shock than coming to YTI:

> I remember the first Sunday I was back at home and I went into my Dad's church [his father is a Missouri Synod Lutheran pastor]. I was like, 'This is the wrong place', 'I'm not supposed to be here.' Just nothing fitted at all. Whether it actually was

> something I thought was wrong or not, after a whole month of being here and questioning and experiencing so many things, to go back to that same routine that I'd been in for my entire life was just a very strange experience . . . When I first came back I thought, 'This will never work. I just can't stay at this church any more.' I had a lot of questions at YTI and as I came back I slowly began to find some answers for myself and now it's somewhere where I'm comfortable again. 'Gary', 1993[23]

One of the most important things that happens for YTI scholars, and what functions as a transitional bridge for them as they return home, is the construction of a 'contrapuntal self'. Drawing on the musical analogy of counterpoint, James Keen suggests that the dialogical, multicultural format of YTI enables scholars to internalize significant encounters with 'the other' and continue these conversations after 'the other' is no longer physically present. Indeed, it may be that the persons who seemed most 'alien' at first become the most significant internal dialogue partners for a lifetime.[24]

Following YTI 1993, we interviewed 'Mike', a black scholar from Chicago who was at the time trying to save his public high school from extinction. We asked Mike to think about the scholars he had missed the most since YTI ended. He named a few, and then smiled and shook his head:

> You know, the person I think I miss the most is 'Rhonda' (aka 'Southern Belle', from Mobile, AL). She came up to me that first week, the evening after the Urban Plunge, and told me that she had once written a paper about Martin Luther King, Jr. I just stared at her and said, 'Rhonda, that's the past. What you and I have to decide is how we're going to relate to each other beginning here and now.' On that final night at YTI, I think I cried harder when I hugged her than I did with anybody else, because I knew how far the two of us had to come to become friends.

YTI as Ecumenical Practice

Mike's experience with Rhonda is a good example of how the ecumenical nature of YTI provides participants with significant encounters with 'otherness'. For most scholars, such encounters are qualitatively different from those that typically occur in their church youth groups. In this final section, we will explore briefly the contours of 'ecumenism' in relation to YTI.

Derived from the Greek word *oikoumene*, the word 'ecumenical' has had multiple meanings throughout the history of the Church. During the period of the early Church described in the New Testament, *oikoumene* referred to the 'whole world' or to the Roman Empire (which was, in effect, 'the whole world' at the time). Gradually, *oikoumene* came to have ecclesial (the whole Church) and ecclesiastical (conciliar) meaning. Only in the twentieth century has this term been used to designate the worldwide missionary outreach of the Church, formal relations between the unity of two or more Christian communions and a spirit of attitude that expresses the consciousness of and desire for Christian unity.[25]

For youth attending YTI, the background and history of the ecumenical movement has not been a pressing concern. In June of 1994, I attended a conference at St John's College (MN) – Ecumenism Among Us – with ten of our 1993 alumni. They were interested to know that these kinds of conversations had been going on for decades, but decided that it was more challenging to live as an ecumenical community rather than merely talk about it. Internal doctrinal debates seemed of secondary importance to the larger questions facing us today. When given a choice, most of the older adults attended a forum entitled 'When Does Dissent Become Unfaithfulness?' Most of the younger folks present – including our alumni – chose a forum called 'What Can Americans Learn From Christians in Other Countries who Live in a More Religiously Pluralistic Society?'

Clearly, the concern expressed by young people today is how to intend the whole world – including the non-human created order – as a part of 'the global household'. It is inappropriate to exclude anyone from this divine economy, and our alumni seemed impatient with Christians who refused in principle to be in communion with others. This attitude extends to adherents of other faith traditions as well, blurring the conventional distinction between 'ecumenical' and 'interfaith'.

Perhaps YTI is best understood from an eschatological perspective. What we are doing, after all, is initiating a movement rather than building an institution. The movement beckons us to stretch beyond what most of us can currently imagine, especially when we consider the entropy of current denominational structures. As one scholar put it, 'After being here at YTI, I can't imagine worshipping all my life in an all-white congregation. It would be so boring!'

YTI is an invitation to be anti-structure, a levelling, transitional experience of 'communitas' in which participants are freed from the roles and routines of everyday life.[26] In this shared subliminal existence, we are freed to create a symbolic universe that transcends the limitations of our provincial social worlds. We become bilingual in the process, and are never quite 'at home' in one place any more. We gather as a company of strangers, and depart as a company of strangers who have shared a foretaste of the Kingdom.

Some scholars have likened YTI to an extended family. If we are 'family', it is one that has been relativized as the source of ultimate loyalty. Jesus instructed his disciples not to place familial loyalty above their loyalty to God (Matthew 10.32–39). In serving God together, a family will often be physically dispersed:

> It will be scattered, and sown, on all sides of geographic, political, chronological, cultural fences. But its members will pray together while they are scattered not unlike Israel in the Diaspora . . . and in this sense, the family which prays together shares life together with all the saints in Christ.[27]

YTI participants have been given roots by their local faith communities and wings by their experience of a catholic church. When 'Dwayne', a 1993 scholar from Billings, Montana, returned to encounter the terrorism of white supremacist groups in his home town, he was emboldened by the solidarity he had recently experienced at YTI. Dwayne joined with other persons of faith in his community to oppose the actions of these hate groups. He and his family placed a menorah in the window of their home to express their solidarity with the Jewish residents of Billings who were being threatened. Dwayne knew how to become part of a community of moral courage and accountability. 'It was,' he says, 'becoming the company of strangers – just like we read about and practised at YTI.'

CHAPTER 10

From Elvis Presley to Quentin Tarantino: Has Film Become the New Rock 'n' Roll?

JOHN ALLAN

The New Rock 'n' Roll?

It's a phrase that, over the last three years, has cropped up again and again in the British popular media. The idea behind it is simple. Popular music is now played out as a major force in the teenage world. It is no longer the prime carrier of meanings, the most important bridge of membership. Instead we have – well, what? The candidates have been numerous.

At the time when alternative British comedians were making the headlines, it was comedy. When Nick Park and other animators began winning Oscars, it was animation. Poetry was briefly (incredibly) touted. But the most prominent candidate, and the most persuasive, has been film. Is it true that young people are now building their culture around movies in the same way that 1950s' teenagers built theirs around rock 'n' roll?

There is a strong body of supporting evidence. Since 1980, cinema audiences have risen steadily right across the Western world – and the increase has been largely among the young. Of all cinema-goers in the UK, 70 per cent are under 25, and the proportion is even higher in America. More than half of all video rentals are to teenagers. In 1990, *Time* magazine reported that 40 per cent of Hollywood's annual profit was coming from just two months of youth-targeted summer releases. In 1996 *Independence Day*, an immensely popular film among young people, brought Fox $746 million, thus becoming, at a stroke, 'the third all-time global theatrical performer'. This would have made Fox the third most successful company – except that in mid-December Paramount released *Beavis and Butthead Do America*. It was the teenage audience for this film that turned it into an unexpectedly massive hit.

No wonder, then, that Australian film scholar Graeme Turner notes: 'The family market that once sustained the film industry has now all but gone, and in its place is a predominantly youthful market. The film industry now depends on pleasing the 14 to 24 age group.'[1]

While this has been happening, the popular music industry has fallen on hard times. Back in the 1960s, all teenagers everywhere listened to the same few records, followed the same basic styles. Now teenage music has splintered into a confusion of subcults; within my youth group, music is no longer a shared interest that binds teenagers together, but a badge of difference that keeps them apart. There is a cynical awareness among young people that the music doesn't 'belong' to them any more – despite the best attempts of independent labels and entrepreneurial club managers, rock has fallen into the hands of big business interests. Pop music academic Simon Frith even begins his book *Music for Pleasure* by stating boldly, 'I am now quite sure that the rock era is over.' He continues:

> People will go on playing and enjoying rock music, of course (though the label is increasingly vague), but the music business is no longer organized around rock, around the selling of records of a particular sort of musical event to young people. The rock era . . . turned out to be a byway in the development of twentieth-century popular music, rather than, as we thought at the time, any kind of mass cultural revolution. Nowadays, rock anthems are used to sell banks and cars. As I write, *Rolling Stone* magazine is celebrating its twentieth anniversary as though it had always meant to be what it has now become – a slick vehicle for delivering the middle-class, middle-aged leisure market to the USA's most conservative corporate advisers.[2]

This may be overstating the case (and was written before the tremendously creative surge in techno music had manifested itself), but is not an uncommon point of view. Some of the excitement has gone out of rock. Heroes last for only five minutes – who worships the memory of Wham or Bros or even Take That? What was once a wild, radical, new teenage musical form is now over 40 years old, and in 1997 the Establishment finally gave Paul McCartney his knighthood.

And so it does, on the face of it, make sense to ask, is film replacing rock 'n' roll as the central teenage mediator of 'meanings'? Certainly, the two forms have always had a symbiotic relationship. If it had not been for the (woefully bad) 1955 movie *Blackboard Jungle*, Bill Haley would never have become a household name around the world. (Significantly, the birth of rock 'n' roll' was heralded by a trail of torn-up movie theatre seats in many different countries, as young audiences reacted violently to the film.) Songs have become massive hits because of their exposure in films (the reissued *Unchained Melody* in 1990, for example, thanks to *Ghost*, or *Love is All Around* for Wet Wet Wet, thanks to *Four Weddings and a Funeral*). Sometimes songs have promoted films – Robin Hood did much better among teenagers than expected, due to the popularity of Bryan Adams and *(Everything I Do,) I Do It For You*. Rock performers have also often made astute use of film opportunities to further their career – from Elvis and his string of formula song-vehicles, through to Madonna's radical exploitation of video as a medium for self-promotion. Given that film and rock have for so long been closely connected, it would seem a natural move for the two simply to change positions, and for cinema to replace rock in its leading role within teenage culture.

In fact, it seems to me, this is not happening. Over the last year, as I have become interested in this question, I have taken the time to conduct informal and unscientific surveys of opinion – among both teenagers and youth workers – in several very different countries that I've visited (Malaysia, France, Poland, Hungary, Germany and Italy) as well as at home in the UK. The results have been remarkably similar.

What people say

Asked whether they spent more time, thought and money on music or film, teenagers everywhere unhesitatingly identified music as much more important to them. Some (particularly in Malaysia and Poland) said that they knew a group of teenagers for whom *videos* were all-important, but it was clear that these young people were not representative of the mainstream. All acknowledged, however, that films were much more important in their thinking and leisure planning than they had been two or three years ago. The films they identified as particularly impressive were mostly blockbusters and these were almost exclusively of American origin. Quite a few in every country had been to see the same movie several times.

Youth workers were more divided in their opinions. The proportions were roughly the same in each country: around 20 per cent claimed that film had, indeed, replaced music in teenage scales of importance, around 40 per cent claimed that music was still the dominant form, and the remaining 40 per cent felt there was no real difference.

The answers to my questions left me with the impression that, while there is not a lot of clarity about what is going on, there is no unambiguous evidence to suggest that film is 'the new rock 'n' roll'. Music refuses to go away, and film does not have the same hold over the teenage imagination as rock 'n' roll had over the teenagers of the 1950s.

There are good reasons, it seems to me, for this being the case. Video recorders have made it possible to bring films home and view them in all sorts of unlikely places without going near a movie theatre; but still film cannot rival the portability of music. The Walkman and the ghetto blaster (not to mention background muzak in shopping arcades) makes music an ever-present possibility in a way that film cannot be. Because film demands a level of concentration that music doesn't (involving eyes as well as ears), it cannot be subliminal 'wallpaper' in quite the same way.

Film costs a lot of money to produce. In 1995, the Motion Picture Association of America announced that its members spent, on average, $36.4 million on producing and $17.7 million on promoting their wares. (This may be a modest estimate: normal marketing expenses are thought to be closer to $25–30 million.) By contrast, part of the perennial appeal of rock music is that almost anybody can get involved at some level – even if only by joining the neighbourhood garage band. Every new 'wave' in rock music history has had the effect of democratizing the music once again. All you needed to play skiffle was a washboard and an acoustic guitar. To form a 'Merseybeat' group in 1963, £200 worth of equipment was more than enough. To play punk, you hardly needed to know any chords. And, since the advent of cheap samplers and sequencers, you can seemingly make your own 'rave' music without any personal musical ability whatsoever. Hollywood seems dauntingly inaccessible; but anybody can dream of playing the Mean Fiddler.

Furthermore, film translates from culture to culture much less easily than music. It is possible for Japanese or Spanish teens to understand what American rock 'n' roll is all about, even when they can't make sense of the lyrics, but movies are unwatchable unless they are dubbed with the local language. Because film deals in propositional meaning much more than music does, it runs into cultural barriers of misunderstanding and misinterpretation much more readily.

Finally, there's the key question of whether or not the world really needs a 'new rock 'n' roll'. The tremendous surge in teenage culture that attended the rise of rock 'n' roll was not produced solely by the music. Rather, the music was a catalyst for a concerted sociological response by teenagers that had been preparing itself for some time – with its roots in the growing enfranchisement of teenagers in the post-war world, the decline in the importance of the family, the growth of the generation gap, the moral questionings left over from the War and so many other factors that have been more than amply documented by the historians of youth culture. Elvis was just an excuse; it was going to happen anyway. There is no evidence to suggest that such conditions are at work in the social situation of Western teenagers today.

I would argue, then, that film is not 'the new rock 'n' roll'; the claim is wildly overstated. Yet, it is clear that film is a tremendous influence on young people – a shaper of their world and a moulder of their imagination – that this influence is growing and that we have probably not paid as much attention to it as we should.

Where it all came from

The first movie producers to realize the potential of the teenage market were probably American International Pictures (AIP), formed in 1952 to supply short feature films for the drive-in theatres. Their attitude was summed up for *Newsweek* by one of their sales directors:

> We'd like to make nice family pictures, but we're in this for the money. If the kids think it's a good picture and the adults don't, that's all right. Seventy-five per cent of the drive-in audiences are under 25, and 70 per cent of our gross comes from drive-in theatres. God bless the whole 5000 of them.[3]

Despite the success of AIP, and other independents, the major studios ignored the teen market. In Europe, the 'pop revolution' of the mid-1960s led to a brief explosion of experimental films aimed at young people, but by the end of the 1960s it all seemed to be on the wane. When George Melly wrote his influential history of 'the pop arts in Britain', *Revolt Into Style*, he pronounced an epitaph on the 'pop style' in film: 'The ideas seem, for the moment at any rate, back under lock and key. The pop manner has become respectable, pop matter is suspect. In the mass media too the revolt has turned into a style.'[4]

Yet, just at that point, everything was suddenly about to change. A Hollywood 'new wave' of directors began to emerge (Stanley Kubrick, Sidney Lumet, John Frankenheimer, Norman Jewison, and others), with their roots in television and a willingness to experiment with new filmic techniques that upset the established conventions and employed the styles with which 1960s young people had grown up. Hot on their heels came the 'movie brats' – the likes of Steven Spielberg, Martin Scorsese, George Lucas and Francis Ford Coppola – who were graduates of film schools and had a much clearer idea than their predecessors of what could and could not be done through the medium of film. Later generations of directors came from an advertising or MTV background.

Bridges were being built to the cultural work that teenagers recognized, and a new sophisticated viewer was emerging:

> The viewers have watched MTV, too, not to mention endless hours of television storytelling and now the entire repertoire of the world cinema on video. It is not so much that these viewers have a short attention span, as critics protest, but rather that they know all the stories already and they are ready to shift their attention to other levels of the film presentation, to glossy colour schemes, rapid-fire editing or dizzying camera movements which challenge their comprehension and intensify their emotional engagement. The narrative may be suggested, evoked, without having to be fully developed; narrative traditions can be merged, mixed and matched, played against each other as new hybrid forms of entertainment emerge.[5]

Interestingly, it was at just this point that the music business started to realize the market potential of older, more educated young people. 1969 was the first year in British history in which LPs outsold singles. In other words, the typical pop record buyer was now the first-year student, rather than the 14- or 15-year-old without much money. Suddenly, every rock band in the country wanted to play student venues.

The important breakthrough in film came with *Jaws* in 1975. The first major blockbuster directed mainly at young people, it was launched alongside a soundtrack album, T-shirts, plastic tumblers, beach towels, blankets, shark costumes, pyjamas, books, games, posters, water pistols, shark-tooth necklaces, and many other 'tie-ins'. The young audience responded (*Jaws* remains today the sixth biggest film of all time) and the major studios belatedly realized that the youthful audience was a lucrative one.

The first important outcome was the 'youth film' phenomenon of the 1980s (*Sixteen Candles*, *The Breakfast Club*, *Ferris Bueller's Day Off*, *Pretty in Pink*, *Heathers*, and many others). Important in their time, these movies aimed to reflect faithfully the styles, language and cultural mores of 1980s America and, as a result, their international impact was limited. Today, their depiction of greed-driven American parenthood seems woefully dated. But directors such as John Hughes and Howard Deutch none the less created some important work within the parochial limitations of the form and, at the very least, sent out the message to young people that Hollywood was interested in courting them.

In the 1990s, Hollywood directors began to realize that films can be successful with teenage audiences without having to focus narrowly and directly on teenage dilemmas (*Batman Forever*, *Jurassic Park*, *Pretty Woman*). As a result, Thomas Schatz argues that three kinds of film are currently being made: the calculated blockbuster, the 'mainstream A-class star vehicle with sleeper hit potential', such as *Look Who's Talking*, and the 'low-cost independent feature targeted for a specific market and with little chance of anything more than cult film status'[6] (an example of this last class would be *Terminator*, which cost only $6 million to make – *Terminator 2*, however, cost ten times as much, thanks to the runaway success of the original).

Schatz claims that this hedge-your-bets strategy allows the industry to make experiments and fine-tune its approach to the 'youth market', which it now sees as vital. Never before has Hollywood devoted so much time, attention, creativity and money to wooing the teenager. Never before has the cinema made such a calculated pitch for the thoughts and dreams of young people.

What does film do to us?

If this is the situation in which our young people are living, then we need to be asking some serious questions. In the rest of this paper I intend to ask three. First, what does film do to us? Second, what messages are present-day films communicating to our young people? And, third, what implications are there for us as youth workers?

Film as a medium

As far back as 1964, Marshall McLuhan was proclaiming that media such as film were changing our view of reality and our ability to confront the world. McLuhan's famous (and very simplistic) phrase was 'The medium is the message'.[7] In other words, the very act of transmitting a story or a message via film, instead of via book or public lecture, changed the nature of what was being transmitted. The medium was not a neutral carrier, but a source of meaning in itself.

Film as a medium has at least five effects on our culture. First, it 'implodes' the world into what McLuhan called a 'global village'. As young people on several different continents watch movies made thousands of miles from their home, they become familiar with products, habits, mannerisms, phrases, attitudes and assumptions that they would never encounter in their home community. These things become part of their world picture and may, in some ways, be more 'real' to them than traditional attitudes that the older generation in their own culture are attempting to impart. The result, says David Wells, is a sense of rootlessness and impoverishment:

> A civilization that is global in its nature is stripped of all the particularities of any one culture. It belongs to no particular time, place or people. It is able to become global *because* it is drained of many of those things that ordinarily constitute particular cultures. It is precisely because modernity belongs to no one that it can belong to everyone, and this is what makes it empty of many of those things to which people in the past have been committed and which gave them a sense of meaning, often of accomplishment.[8]

Elsewhere in the same book, Wells remarks that life in the city has the effect of eroding differences between people:

> City life requires the kind of friendliness that allows us to cohabit with the mass ethic. It is typically assumed that this sort of friendliness must be divested of moral or religious truth, since it is difficult for our society to see how judgements about truth and morals can escape the charge of social bigotry. And so we settle for the kind of friendliness within which all absolutes perish either for lack of interest or because of the demands of the social etiquette.[9]

To enjoy the typical modern movie, to make sense of its imaginative world, one has constantly to suspend one's particular viewpoints and values in order to identify with those of the film. There is nothing wrong in this; all art demands such an engagement, and imaginatively entering into someone else's thought world is an educative experience. However, when the viewpoint with which we are invited to identify is virtually the same in movie after movie – the pared-down, stripped-to-essentials, vaguely spiritual but endlessly tolerant outlook of the bland twentieth-century global village – it becomes more and more difficult to retain any sense of our own particular values. No wonder so many Christian young people believe one thing and live another – they are being taught what to believe by the Church and how to live by the movies.

Second, film provides an experience of entering another world, a 'hermetically sealed universe, unwinding by itself, unconcerned by the presence of an audience' (to quote Laura Mulvey).[10] Watching a movie demands our full attention, and during the exercise our senses are totally absorbed in what is going on. This (as we'll see later) gives the experience a peculiar imaginative power of its own. A well-made movie can decisively alter our view of reality (witness the important role of Leni Riefenstahl's propaganda films in 'selling' Nazism to Germany). Film is a much more persuasive medium than music. Because it tells a story, it presents a more complete picture of reality and so is always implicitly arguing for a verdict.

Third, film is fundamentally a non-rational medium. It does not advance arguments as books or radio programmes do (and when it is misused to do this, the results can be woeful – as in, for example, the earliest range of evangelical *Fact and Faith* films). It recommends its view of the world by creating an intense sensory experience in which our critical faculties may well be lulled to sleep. (For example, at the end of *An Officer and a Gentleman*, we ought to be seriously unconvinced about the realistic prospects of the future relationship of Richard Gere and Debra Winger, but we don't ask those kinds of questions because we are so stirred by the dramatic final scene in which he sweeps her into his arms and out of the factory. We should be more worried about the easy forgiveness *Fatal Attraction* provides for its erring male hero, and concerned about the wrong done to his one-night pick-up, but by the end of the film she has been demonized into a vengeful monster and so we let the moral question slide.)

The best film-makers are often extremely vague about what they are trying to do. It isn't so much a matter of deliberate creation as of tentatively feeling towards a 'truth'. Here, for example, is Scorsese on *Raging Bull*:

> Bobby and I never really intended to do that kind of thing, but we did it by making this inside thing that we know. We did it as honestly as we know how. There's no point in doing anything else.
>
> At a certain point in your life you realize something's there that's a part of your background, part of your make-up. That you *can't deny*. You have to be honest with that. You have to deal with what are called the 'negative' aspects. You have to claw your way through them.[11]

There is one extremely violent line in *Taxi Driver* that embarrasses Scorsese: 'A lot of famous guys come over to me and say, "I love it when you say that line" . . . It's amazing. I'm embarrassed, because it slipped out by accident.'

When intentions are as unclear and methods are as imprecise as this, we need to realize that we cannot make easy, simple statements about the 'message' of a film. Frequently the experience of movie-watching will be an ambiguous, unsettling one. Good films cannot be easily pigeon-holed. A recent case in point is *Kids*, banned from public exhibition in Britain. The film deals with serious themes: the consequences of promiscuity, gender difference, peer acceptance, the treating of other human beings as pleasure objects. It deals with these themes in a chilling way, evacuating all sympathy from the characters so as to prevent easy identification with them, presenting sexual encounters as acts of aggression rather than with any attractiveness. It attempts to be authentic. Larry Clark claimed that:

> most teenage films are . . . written by 40-year-old people and all the words coming out of these kids' mouths are the words of a 40-year-old writer. [*Kids*] was written by one of the kids in this subculture. I got access to the reality of these kids. This was an inside job. This was real. I wanted to make a movie . . . that kids would see and say, 'For once they made a film that's not bullshit.'

Yet, the unease with the film is well-founded. The presence of a 52-year-old director cannot be discounted quite so easily, even when the scriptwriter is 19. The lingering, unemotional camera-work suggests an underlying voyeuristic impulse that is never quite admitted and which creates an unsettling subtext to the movie. Its ultimate impact is self-contradictory.

As feeling and atmosphere count for so much in the 'truth' of a film, it is not surprising that nostalgia is such an important selling-point for the movies. This can include both historical recreations (*Braveheart*, *Rob Roy*, *Michael Collins*) and reproductions of great works of a literary tradition. At the time of writing, New Yorkers can see four new Shakespeare films on current release: *Hamlet*, *Twelfth Night*, *Richard III*, and *Romeo and Juliet*. 1996 saw a craze for Jane Austen (*Emma*, *Sense and Sensibility*). However, it is important to note that the audiences flocking to these films are not drawn by the timeless truths contained in great literature; instead, it's precisely the opposite – they want to escape into a make-believe historical world of nostalgic simplicity.

In his controversial book *Technopoly*, Neil Postman[12] argues that we are experiencing within our culture a collision of different ways of learning and knowing. The book-based, analytical tradition on which education has traditionally been founded is now coming into conflict with the sensory orientation of the TV learning style. What this can produce is a dangerous naivety about what can and can't be believed.

Film critic Judith Williamson observes, 'Films tend to make you feel that the events and people pictured could *only* have been as they are shown – and this is not only true of Hollywood films, it applies almost as much to most of the "avant-garde"'.[13] The power of the spectacle is such that we believe it too easily. Oliver Stone may well have said that 'The movie audience does not generally take a movie literally. And if they do, they need an education.' But that didn't stop Congress calling for a re-examination of the Kennedy shooting when *JFK* came out.

Fourth, film tells its story in a different way from a book (or even television). It presents us with a sequence of changing scenes, constantly switching the point of view from one to another, and it leaves us to work out the connections between the different scenes that are being shown. There is (usually) no authorial presence; we have the responsibility for working out the puzzle.

> The structure of film narrative is such that its meaning has to be actively constructed by the viewers as they watch . . . Each shot in a film is continually involved in constructing the relationships which will help the film make sense – relationships between one shot and the next, one sequence and its adjacent sequences, and so on . . . This deferral of meaning, the closing of gaps by the viewers, means that they drive the narrative forward in order to understand what they have seen.[14]

This process mirrors the way in which modern people experience life. Alvin Toffler has remarked that we live in a 'blip culture':

> Instead of receiving long, related 'strings' of ideas, organized or synthesized for us, we are increasingly exposed to short, modular blips of information – ads, commands, theories, shreds of news, truncated bits and bobs that refuse to fit neatly into our pre-existing mental files . . .
>
> Instead of merely receiving our mental model of reality, we are now compelled to invent it and continually reinvent it. This places an enormous burden on us.[15]

If the media we use do carry their own implicit 'messages', then one outcome of watching lots of movies may be a predisposition to believe that you can't believe any of the 'big stories', whether Christianity, Marxism or Islam – you simply have to move through life as an independently judging neutral, forming your personal view of reality and creating your personal values as you travel along. The individual is the only source of authority:

> The camera itself is an apparatus that embodies a theory of reality, an ideology, because it sees the world as the object of a single individual's point of view. We claim to see and possess the world as individuals – a view not held before the Renaissance but increasingly demonstrated in nineteenth-century art and entertainment.[16]

But, finally, we also need to note that film is a narcissistic medium. It invites us to witness passively, to identify with the spectacle it is presenting and become absorbed by it. And so (much more than the written work) it encourages the problem of 'fiction addiction' – habitual escape into fantasy as a way of avoiding any real confrontation with reality. At a time when too many young people in Western culture are looking for easy escape routes from the tensions of their lives, it offers a much more complete, absorbing distraction than rock music ever did.

To see the entertainment system as a capitalist conspiracy is madness, yet there is something taking place – something big and seething, in which the desire to be diverted occasionally is becoming a full-blown obsession with escape through entertainment. In the 1970s, American teachers reported that previously promising college students had started to drop out of their classes in order to be able to follow the born-again torrid daytime soap operas – people sacrificing real lives because the fictional lives of others seemed more immediately, vitally important. As the world opens up and gets bigger, we close up and feel smaller, and turn our troubled minds and stomachs from the torments of factual comments to the quarrels of fictional streets; as the world becomes a global village, we become global village idiots, sleepwalking through a life where our best friends are soap opera characters, and our leaders are, too.

> We are heading towards a time when real life will only be understood through entertainment . . . Information not presented as entertainment will not be absorbed – the rise of 'faction' shows this. A people who cannot digest anything but fiction – the strained babyhood of communications – . . . are in danger of mass stupidity – of passing on to their children a world divided strictly into entertainers and audiences, in which the bringer of boring knowledge will not be welcome at all.[17]

What are the movies telling us?

So much for the general impact of film as a medium. We also need to be aware that the movies young people watch have specific messages to deliver too. What are the movies telling us?

To decode the 'message' of a movie isn't an easy job. As we have seen above, often even the best film-makers are remarkably unclear about exactly what they are trying to achieve. In the work of, for example, Hitchcock – or, more recently, Tarantino – it is easy to spot personal obsessions, recurrent dilemmas and so on, of which the director is clearly quite unaware. And the 'meaning' of films can be altered crucially by commercial concerns. The scriptwriter of *Four Weddings and a Funeral* clearly had a sequence in which characters who are desperately preparing for a marriage ceremony utter nothing but the word 'fuck', repeatedly, for the first few minutes of the film, but to gain entry to the American market, he cheerfully suggested changing the word to 'bugger', which meant that the crudity remained but the point was lost.

Sam Goldwyn was famous for remarking that, if film-makers wanted to send a message, they should go to Western Union. Movies were about entertainment, not portentous statement. Yet movies do have things to say – things that help to shape the world view of their audiences – and youth workers need to be aware of what these are.

There is a lot to be said on this issue, but here I want to make just five simple points. First, the 'message' of today's films tends to reflect our own society's unconfronted prejudices. In a famous *Screen* article in 1975, Laura Mulvey showed just how deeply sexist attitudes control our expectations of film. Narrative film has conventions and formulas that encourage the 'male gaze', putting us all in the position of male voyeur. Most key roles go to men (72 per cent of all speaking parts in Hollywood films between 1989 and 1994). The female body is presented in quite a different way from the male body, and women are rarely, if ever, given roles of true power. (*Thelma and Louise* at first seems to be an exception, but is it? The film-makers could not decide about the ending, and so screened two alternatives, asking audiences to vote for the preferred one. Overwhelmingly, viewers chose the one in which the two women are punished for their exploits by death.)

Films that appear to criticize Western imperialism don't always. Edward Said has written of the 'anger' that pervades Oliver Stone's *Salvador*, Francis Ford Coppola's *Apocalypse Now* and Constantin Costa-Gavras's *Missing* – but it isn't enough:

> Yet all these works . . . argue that the source of the world's significant life and action is in the West, whose representatives seem at liberty to visit their fantasies and philanthropies upon a mind-deadened Third World. In this view, the outlying regions of the world have no life, history, or culture to speak of, no independence or integrity worth representing without the West.[18]

Said argues that such films dramatize a conflict, for the purposes of entertainment, but ultimately lack 'the political willingness to take seriously the alternatives to imperialism, among them the existence of other cultures and societies'.

The sheer size of Hollywood dictates that American culture will predominate in world film. When *Crocodile Dundee* came to America, it opened in 900 cinemas on the same night – which is 200 more cinemas than exist in the whole of Australia. Not surprisingly, within 12 days it had already earned more in the USA than it had earned in six months in Australia – and it had been the biggest box-office success in Australian history.

In Britain in 1996, *Independence Day* made $68.6 million, in Germany, $61 million, but these figures are dwarfed by the $306.2 million it made domestically in America. Not surprisingly, Hollywood dominates the world; 1996's top ten films in Germany included only three local products (*Werner*, *Mannerpension*, *Hera Linds*). In Britain there was only one: *Trainspotting*.

This does not mean that America is about to conquer the world. Michael Medved has pointed out that the percentage of revenue from foreign sales to American studios is constantly increasing, and this will mean that American producers have to pay more and more attention to the demands of a *world* market. (In 1980, only 30 per cent of revenues came from foreign sales; in 1994, for the first time in history, more than half did so.)

This means that a large quantity of highly influential film is coming from one source, and that therefore there are likely to be blind spots, unwarranted cultural assumptions and a persuasive homogeneity of our world view, as long as the predominant characteristics of one nation's film products are not being challenged in a healthy way by perspectives from other national cinemas. Films will tend to keep on perpetuating the same kind of approach to life that has conventionally brought success.

Second, films today are presenting to teenagers a 'message' about the real world that is only partially a true picture. Medved speaks stridently and bitterly about this:

> Thirty-two per cent of all Americans described themselves as born-again Christians, 52 per cent of African-Americans – 52 per cent – do you see that a lot on TV? Do you see that a lot in the movies? All you see in portrayals of African-Americans are thugs and drugs . . .
>
> There is one occupational group responsible for 40 per cent of all murders on television. That is a higher percentage than members of the Mafia or any other group. Do you know what occupation group that is? Businessmen! . . .
>
> I actually went to some trouble to go to the FBI's Bureau of Crime Statistics. The actual statistic is about one half of 1 per cent of all murders are committed by businessmen, not 40 per cent. And almost all of those are domestic tragedies. This is absurd. It is not reality. Hollywood doesn't reflect reality.[19]

Medved points out that by 1994 there were already four different movies in existence about the lady who had earlier that year cut off her husband's penis. 'This is reality? . . . I mean is this the most over-reported story in the twentieth century or what?' Film's focus on spectacle, its need to draw attention to itself, constantly propels it in the direction of the unusual, the freak, the extreme. It gives us a fascination with unusual circumstances and dramatic cases. (As a result, self-dramatizing individuals queue up to expose their unusual personal inadequacies to Oprah Winfrey and Ricki Lake on prime time television – and the rest of us tune in to watch them.)

Third, the realistic cinema of the early twentieth century has given way to a cinema of 'magical realism' in which the boundaries of truth and fantasy are blurred. Films invite us to play around with the borders of reality (which is what makes the 'faction' films of directors like Oliver Stone so potentially dangerous). Gene Veith contrasts a 'modern' film like *Citizen Kane* – in which reality is presented 'from a number of different points of view as a way of fixing its meaning' – with 'post-modern' films like *Blue Velvet*, *Blade*

Runner, *Roger Rabbit* or *The Purple Rose of Cairo*, which set up 'different worlds, all occupying the same space' and ask characters to discover which world they are actually in.[20] Veith connects this to the cry of despair at the heart of all post-modern art: the bleak message that there is no such thing as 'objective' reality; that we all create our realities for ourselves, that we cannot accept anyone else's 'truth' about the world because our own 'truth' is likely to be essentially different.

Fourth, because of this openness to alternative realities, modern film is prepared to play about with spiritual possibilities in a way that was not acceptable even two decades ago. The underlying 'Hollywood Hinduism' of films like *Star Wars* and the unresolved probings of films like *Flatliners* communicate a vaguely mystical awareness that, it seems to me, passes on two messages to today's teenagers. First, 'there's something else out there', but, second, 'you can't be certain what it is'.

We ignore this influence of modern film at our peril. 'What good does it do us,' asks Terry Mattingly, 'to know systematic theology, to know our Church's moral teachings or to have mastered a host of other religious disciplines, if we cannot recognize when our culture beams theological and moral questions to us in the guise of entertainment?'

Fifth, and perhaps even more importantly, modern cinema is communicating a style of decision making – a message that absolute truths cannot be discovered in one place, at one time, but that partial truths are all that can be picked up along the journey. Jean-Luc Godard was once asked what the 'moral' of one of his films was. He famously replied, '*Le moral, c'est le travelling*' – '*le travelling*' being a technical cinematographer's word for what the camera does when it pans round a whole scene slowly. In other words, the only truth you will learn from my film is that which you pick up for yourself as you watch it. No one else can decide your views or inform your mind – you must do it alone.

Confronted years later by the girl he has seduced, Indiana Jones responds, 'I did what I did.' There is no other defence: we are each locked into our own private worlds of motivation and value, and we cannot be judged from the outside by anyone else. The important thing is to be true to yourself, not to become locked into anyone else's system; this is the point of *Trainspotting*: 'Choose life. Choose a job. Choose a career. Choose a family. Choose a big television. Choose washing machines, cars, compact disc players, and electrical tin openers. Choose sitting on the couch watching mind-numbing, spirit-crushing game shows.'

What are the implications for youthwork?

For Christian youth workers, the implications are not difficult to work out. Film may not be a replacement for rock 'n' roll in its power to constitute the teenage mindset, but, none the less, it is an important medium, rapidly growing in its influence over the imaginations and opinions of those with whom we are working. Several things follow.

First, we need to know what is happening, and attempt to understand it. Without being negative about modern cinema, we need to see clearly the mechanisms it unconsciously uses to shape and inform the spirit of the age. We need to see how young people's prejudices are being confirmed, and where their critical faculties are being lulled to sleep, and we need to be prepared to challenge those effects.

Second, we need to foster a critical spirit in the young people we work with. Part of our work needs to focus on educating the minds of teenagers to confront the modern cinema with intelligent questions and an independence of mind. If they are to survive the onslaught of the modern media, young people need to develop an acute awareness of the ways in which they are being persuaded and the half-truths they are being told.

Third, we need to challenge the 'spectator' lifestyle of so many young people, which results in a passive acceptance of whatever the entertainment factory is churning out this week. The more our culture saps the vitality and creativity of young people, turning them into exploited consumers rather than initiative-takers, the more the Gospel needs to be good news that frees them into a fuller, more challenging, stretching life.

Fourth, we need to harness the imaginative power of today's cinema, and its capacity to evoke unforgettable images, as a tool in apologetics and evangelism. The fictions on which young people feed – from *Robocop* to *Chariots of Fire* – provide them with a stock of mental pictures that we can use to illustrate, argue or contrast in presenting the Gospel to them. If film is a powerful language for young people today, then youth workers need to learn to speak it.

Notes

Chapter 1

1 See Elkind's *The Hurried Child* (Addison-Wesley, 1981 and 1988) and *All Grown Up and No Place To Go* (Addison-Wesley, 1984).

2 I think of and teach research as the second of nine stages of youth ministry after the first task of developing a strong support base of pastoral endorsement, an adult committee and a varied leadership team.

3 J. L. McKenchnic, *et al.* (Eds), *Webster's New Twentieth-century Dictionary*, 2nd edition (William Collins, 1979).

Chapter 2

1 G. Keillor, *Lake Wobegon Days* (Penguin, 1985), p. 17.

2 Cited in D. Hollinger, 'The Church As Apologetic', in T. R. Phillips and D. L. Okholm (Eds), *Christian Apologetics in the Post-modern World* (InterVarsity Press, 1995), p. 185.

3 Hollinger.

4 See M. H. Senter III, *The Coming Revolution in Youth Ministry* (Victor Books, 1992).

5 See J. E. Reed and R. Prevost, *A History of Christian Education* (Broadman & Holman, 1993).

6 J. B. Erickson, 'American Youth Organizations: An Etiological Approach', MA thesis (University of Minnesota, 1968).

7 Peter M. Senge, *The Fifth Discipline* (Doubleday, 1990), pp. 7–26. The other disabilities include 'I am my position', 'The enemy is out *there*', 'The illusion of taking charge', 'Fixation on events', 'The parable of the boiled frog', and 'The myth of the management team'.

8 Peter L. Benson, '40 Developmental Assets', *Assets*, Search Institute, Autumn 1996, p. 11.

Chapter 3

1 See D. Borgman, 'A History of American Youth Ministry', in W. Benson and M. Senter (Eds), *The Complete Book of Youth Ministry* (Moody Press, 1987); M. Senter, *The Coming Revolution in Youth Ministry and Its Impact on the Church* (Victor Books, 1992); and P. Ward, *Growing Up Evangelical: Youthwork and the making of a subculture* (SPCK, 1996).

2 See Senter.

3 S. Gerali, 'Paradigms in the Contemporary Church that Reflect Generational Values', in P. Ward (Ed.), *The Church and Youth Ministry*, (Lynx Communications, 1995).

4 W. Strauss and N. Howe, *Generations: The history of America's future 1584 to 2069* (William Morrow and Company Inc., 1991); M. Blau, 'Child Exclusive: . . . and now Generation Xers are Parents', *Child* (1995).

5 N. Howe, and B. Strauss, *13th Gen: Abort, retry, ignore, fail?* (Vintage Books, 1993).

6 Strauss and Howe, 1991.

7 Strauss and Howe, 1991.

8 Strauss and Howe, 1991.

9 Strauss and Howe, 1991, p. 342.

10 Blau.

11 See Gerali.

12 Howe and Strauss, 1993.

13 G. Celente, 'Trends 2000: How to prepare for the profit from the changes of the 21st century' (unpublished manuscript), originally published in *Psychology Today*, January/February 1997, Vol. 30, No. 1, p. 46.

14 Celente.

15 Celente.

16 S. Gerali and J. Gerali, 'Cross-gender Counselling', in D. Elliott and G. Olsen (Eds), *Breaking the Gender Barrier in Youth Ministry* (Victor Books, 1994).

17 W. Laqueur, 'Once More with Feeling: Post-modernism and millennialism', in *Society*, November/December 1995, Vol. 33, No. 1, p. 32.

18 N. Merchant and P. Dupuy, 'Multicultural Counseling and Qualitative Research: Shared worldview and skills', *Journal of Counseling and Development*, July/August 1996, Vol. 74, pp. 537–41; D. Offer, E. Ostrov, K. Howard and R. Atkinson, *The Teenage World: Adolescents' self-image in ten countries* (Plenum Medical Press, 1988).

19 M. White, *The Material Child: Coming of age in Japan and America* (The Free Press, 1993).

20 CyberEdge, on the Worldwide Web, 1996.

21 J. Schwartz, 'A Terminal Obsession', *The Washington Post*, March 27, 1994, Section F, p. 4.
22 O. Guinness, *Fit Bodies, Fat Minds* (Baker Book House, 1994).
23 H. Rheingold, *Virtual Reality* (Touchstone Books, 1991).
24 CyberEdge.
25 Rheingold, p. 346.
26 W. Laqueur; S. Grenz, 'Post-modernism and the Future of Evangelical Theology', in D. Dockery (Ed.), *The Challenge of Post-modernism: An evangelical engagement* (Victor Books, 1995).
27 P. Rosenau, *Post-modernism and the Social Sciences: Insights, inroads, and intrusions* (Princeton University Press, 1992).
28 Grenz.
29 Z. Bauman, *Intimations of Post-modernity* (Routledge, 1992).
30 Rosenau.
31 R. A. Shweder, 'Divergent Rationalities', in D. Fiske and R. Shweder, *Metatheory in Social Sciences* (University of Chicago Press, 1986).
32 Celente.
33 Laqueur.
34 Grenz.
35 Celente.
36 Celente.
37 F. Warner, 'Advertising: Churches turn to marketing plans to spread their spiritual message', *The Wall Street Journal*, April 17, 1995, Section B, p. 4.
38 R. Ostling, 'The Church Search', *Time*, April 1993, pp. 44–9; W. C. Roof, *A Generation of Seekers: The spiritual journey of the baby boom generation* (HarperCollins, 1993); C. Russell, *The Master Trend: How the baby boom generation is remaking America* (Plenum Press, 1993); R. Luce, 'How we can reach Generation X', *Charisma*, September 1994, pp. 20–7; A. Tapia, 'Reaching the First Post-Christian Generation', *Christianity Today*, September 1994, pp. 18–33.
39 Laqueur.

Chapter 4

1 This question is taken from the title of a book in the Introductory Studies in Philosophy of Education series: R. Straughan, *Can We Teach Children to be Good?* (Allen & Unwin, 1982).
2 Straughan, p. 14.
3 R. Hersh, J. Miller and G. Fielding, *Models of Moral Education: An appraisal* (Longman, 1980), p. 2.
4 See A. J. Ayer, *Language, Truth and Logic* (Gollancz, 1936).
5 Straughan, pp. 36 and 38.

6 D. Carr, *Educating the Virtues* (Routledge, 1991), pp. 210–14.
7 P. Baelz, *Ethics and Belief* (Sheldon Press, 1977), p. 86.
8 Carr, p. 228.
9 Carr, pp. 191–231.
10 Baelz, p. 77.
11 Baelz, p. 86.
12 R. S. Peters, *Ethics and Education* (Allen & Unwin, 1966), p. 121.
13 Straughan, p. 76.
14 A. S. Neill, *Summerhill* (Penguin, 1968), pp. 110–11.
15 J. Wilson, *A New Introduction to Moral Education* (Cassell, 1990), p. 43.
16 Straughan, p. 56.
17 Baelz, p. 111.
18 A. Kolnai, *Erroneous Conscience*, quoted in Straughan, pp. 59–60.
19 Baelz, p. 19.
20 Hersh, *et al.*, p. 5.
21 Baelz, p. 31.
22 Baelz, p. 34.
23 See R. M. Hare, *Freedom and Reason* (Oxford University Press, 1963).
24 N. Cooper, 'Further thoughts on oughts and wants', in G. Mortimer (Ed.), *Weakness of Will* (Macmillan, 1971), p. 225.
25 Straughan, p. 14 (see also p. 10).
26 Carr, p. 259.
27 R. Gill, *Moral Communities* (University of Exeter Press, 1992), p. 14.
28 J. P. White, *Towards a Compulsory Curriculum* (Routledge & Kegan Paul, 1973), pp. 48–9.
29 See J. Shaver and W. Strong, *Facing Value Decisions: Rationale building for teachers* (Wadsworth, 1976).
30 See L. Kohlberg, 'Stages of Moral Development as a Basis for Moral Education', in C. M. Beck, B. S. Crittenden and E. V. Sullivan (Eds), *Moral Education* (Newman Press, 1971).
31 R. Hersh, D. Paolitto and J. Reimer, *Promoting Moral Growth – from Piaget to Kohlberg* (Longman, 1979), p. 64.
32 Carr, p. 166.
33 C. Gilligan, *In a Different Voice* (Harvard University Press, 1982).
34 Hersh, *et al.*, p. 135.
35 Straughan, p. 87.
36 See F. Newmann, *Education for Citizen Action: Challenge for secondary curriculum* (McCutchan, 1975).
37 Hersh, *et al.*, p. 198.
38 Carr, p. 223.
39 N. Tate, School Curriculum and Assessment Authority, *BBC News Extra* (3 January, 1997).
40 Gill, p. 17.

41 See W. Kay and L. Francis, *Drift from the Churches: Attitudes towards Christianity during childhood and adolescence* (University of Wales Press, 1996).
42 A. MacIntyre, *After Virtue* (Duckworth, 1981), p. 263.
43 See S. Hauerwas and W. Willimon, *Resident Aliens: Life in the Christian colony* (Abingdon, 1989).
44 D. Bass (Ed.), *Practising Our Faith: A way of life for a searching people* (Jossey-Bass, 1997), p. 5.
45 D. C. Richter, *Roots and Wings: Practising theology with youth*, paper given at The Second Conference on Youth Ministry, Mansfield College, Oxford, January 1997, pp. 6–7.
46 Gill, pp. 22–3.

Chapter 5

1 R. N. Bellah, *The Broken Covenant: American civil religion in time of trial* (University of Chicago Press, 1992) p. 81.
2 See N. E. Copeland Jr, *Great Games for City Kids* (Youth Specialties/Zondervan, 1991), pp. 19–20.
3 See N. E. Copeland Jr, *The Heroic Revolution: A new agenda for urban youthwork* (Winston-Derek, 1995), pp. ix–xi.
4 'The Salvation Army Song', to the tune of 'The Campbells are coming'. See T. Dowley (Ed.), *Eerdman's Handbook to the History of Christianity* (Eerdmans, 1977), p. 518.
5 E. Isichei, *A History of Christianity in Africa* (Eerdmans, 1995), p. 1.
6 See Copeland, 1995, pp. 7–8.
7 Nathan A. Scott, *Mirrors of Man in Existentialism* (Abingdon, 1978), p. 136.
8 See Copeland, 1995, pp. 2–4.
9 See D. Martin, *Tongues of Fire: The explosion of Protestantism in Latin America* (Blackwell, 1990), p. 180.
10 Copeland, 1995, p. 192.
11 Arnobius of Sicca, 'The Case Against the Pagans', G. E. McCracken (Trans.), *Ancient Christian Writers*, Vol. 1 (The Newman Press, 1949), p. 58.
12 Copeland, 1995, p. 195.
13 See Copeland, 1995, pp. 193–194.
14 See J. Edwards, 'Christian Charity; or The Duty of Charity to the Poor, Explained and Enforced', *The Works of President Edwards*, Research and Source Work Series, Vol. 5, No. 271 (Burt Franklin, 1968), p. 399.
15 Edwards, pp. 400–1 (Edwards' emphasis).
16 Copeland, 1995, p. 193.
17 Copeland, 1995, p. 202.

18 B. W. Bacon, *Non-resistance: Christian or pagan?* (Yale University Press, 1918), p. 26.
19 Leroy H. Pelton, *The Psychology of Non-violence* (Pergamon Press, 1974), p. 16.
20 N. E. Copeland Jr, 'The Relevance of the Christian Tradition of Non-violent Resistance as a Strategic Premise for Implementing Social Change in Urban America' (second draft, MA thesis in Christian social ethics, Gordon Conwell Theological Seminary, 1993).
21 Copeland, 1995, p. 202.
22 E. Troeltsch, and Olive Wyon (Trans.), *The Social Teaching of the Christian Churches* (1912; reprint John Knox Press, 1992), p. 59.
23 'Society's soul' refers to that within every society that, if appealed to correctly, can cause guilt to fall on the entire society and move it towards paradigmatic change.
24 Troeltsch, p. 107.
25 See Copeland, 1995, pp. 203–4.
26 G. Wil, 'The Wilde Wild West', *The Washington Post*, August 1, 1982.
27 Aristotle, 'Nicomachean Ethics', II.i.4–5, H. Rackam (Trans.), *Loeb Classical Library*, Vol. 19 (Harvard University Press, 1926, reprinted 1982), p. 731.
28 Copeland, 1995, p. 206.
29 See S. Callahan, *In Good Conscience: Reason and emotion in moral decision making* (Harper, 1991), pp. 95, 97 and 98.
30 Callahan, p. 99.
31 Callahan, p. 95.
32 Callahan, p. 103.
33 Copeland, 1995, p. 207.
34 Plato's discussion with Glaucon is found in B. C. Birch and L. L. Rassmussen, *Bible and Ethics in the Christian Life*, p. 43. Original source not located at time of publication.
35 Isichei, p. 326.
36 Copeland, 1995, pp. 204–5.
37 W. Rauschenbusch, *A Theology for the Social Gospel* (Abingdon, 1987), p. 179 – originally published in 1917 by Macmillan.
38 Quotation from Walter Rauschenbusch, in P. M. Minus, *Walter Rauschenbusch: American reformer* (Macmillan, 1988), p. 56.
39 See A. Toynbee, *A Study of Human History* (Oxford University Press, 1972), pp. 97 and Chapter 13. See also commentary on Toynbee – N. Gingrich, *To Renew America* (HarperCollins, 1995), pp. 22–3.
40 See Copeland, 1995, pp. 211–12.

Chapter 6

1 A. Pollack (Ed.), *A Citizens' Inquiry – The Opsahl Report on Northern Ireland* (The Liliput Press, 1993), p. 104.

2 J. McGarry and B. O'Leary, *Explaining Northern Ireland* (Blackwell Press, 1995), p. 188.

3 J. Whyte, *Interpreting Northern Ireland* (Clarendon Press, 1990), p. 27.

4 D. Morrow, *The Churches and Inter-community Relationships* (University of Ulster, 1991), p. 123.

5 Morrow, p. 124.

6 Morrow's research demonstrates how cultural identity in Northern Ireland is inextricably linked to religion and the Church.

7 'Cross-community work' generally denotes planned programmes that aim to increase trust and understanding between the two traditions – Protestants and Catholics. This work usually involves preparation of leaders, preparation of participants, initial contact, usually discussions regarding the conflict and ways to build trust and understanding or work together on agreed activities. The term 'community relations work' encompasses many types of work that aim to improve community relations work, for example, justice and civil rights work, community development work, cultural traditions work, reconciliation work. Often the two terms are interchangeable in certain contexts.

8 Morrow, p. 119.

9 See S. Bruce, *God Save Ulster* (Oxford University Press, 1986), p. 249.

10 The Evangelical Contribution on Northern Ireland (ECONI) Conference, 'God, State and Nation', 22 November, 1996.

11 Morrow, p. 122.

12 Another consideration is that the minority/majority balance in Northern Ireland has been a more difficult ratio for a negotiable solution. When the minority is relatively small, accommodation has usually been easier to find. Alternatively, when the majority of a colonized country rises up seeking independence, then the minority, the powerholders, find it increasingly difficult to continue to oppress the majority of the people in these modern times. Northern Ireland is a little different, with the latest figures showing it to be roughly 40.6 per cent Catholic and 55.6 per cent Protestant.

13 However, I believe more churches are becoming involved in the Prayers for Christian Unity and 176 congregations participated in ECONI Sunday in 1996. ECONI is again a parachurch organization, not essentially a church structure. ECONI 'seeks to promote a greater understanding and application of Biblical principles in the Northern Ireland situation'. It noted that in 1995, approximately 35,000 church members have participated in the ECONI Sunday worships, which

challenge Christians with the message of reconciliation. There are established churches involved in interchurch activities, but all too few, as the *Churches Working Together* directory can testify.

14 See P. Weinreich. For a summary of methods using identity structural analysis and its implications for studying Northern Ireland, see 'Socio-psychological Maintenance of Ethnicity in Northern Ireland – a commentary', *The Psychologist*, Vol. 5, pp. 345–6.

Chapter 7

1 Based on the King James and NEB translations.
2 K. Gandhi and D. Oakley, *The Asian And African-Caribbean Youth Project: The way forward* (Oxfordshire County Council, 1996), p. 1.
3 OFSTED, *Recent Research on the Achievements of Ethnic Minority Pupils* (HMSO, 1996), p. 80.
4 T. Modood, S. Beishon and S. Virdee, *Changing Ethnic Identities* (Policy Studies Institute, 1994), p. 119.
5 See P. Ward, 'Christian Relational Care', Chapter 1 in P. Ward (Ed.), *Relational Youthwork* (Lynx Communications, 1995).
6 M. Angelou, *Conversations with Maya Angelou* (Cox and Wyman, 1989).
7 B. McGinn (Ed.), *Ephrem the Syrian: Hymns* (Paulist Press, 1989).
8 P. Grant and R. Patel (Eds), *A Time to Speak* (Russell Press, 1990), p. 12.
9 T. Lane, *The Lion Concise Book of Christian Thought* (Lion Publishing, 1986), p. 227.

Chapter 8

1 J. Lewis, *Labour and Love* (Blackwell, 1986).
2 T. Apter, *Why Women Don't Have Wives: Professional success and motherhood* (Macmillan, 1985).
3 E. Storkey, *What's Right with Feminism?* (SPCK, 1985, 1994); M. Furlong, *A Dangerous Delight* (SPCK, 1991).
4 V. Beechey and E. Whitelegg (Eds), *Women in Britain Today* (Open University Press, 1986) and S. Llewelyn and K. Osborne, *Women's Lives* (Routledge, 1990).
5 M. Coats, *Women's Education* (Open University Press, 1994).
6 M. J. Davidson and R. J. Burke, *Women in Management* (Paul Chapman, 1994).
7 S. Dex, *Women's Attitudes Towards Work* (Macmillan, 1988).
8 A. Furnham and B. Stacy, *Young People's Understanding of Society* (Routledge, 1991).
9 S. Irwin, *Rites of Passage* (UCL Press, 1995).

10 B. G. Worrall, *The Making of the Modern Church* (SPCK, 1993) and Storkey, 1985.
11 W. K. Kay and L. J. Francis, *Drift from the Churches* (University of Wales Press, 1996).
12 S. Gill, *Women and the Church of England* (SPCK, 1994).
13 A. Holdsworth, *Out of the Doll's House* (BBC, 1988).
14 D. J. Pawson, *Leadership is Male* (Highland Books, 1988).
15 Furlong.
16 C. Renzetti and D. J. Curran, *Women, Men and Society* (Allyn and Bacon, 1992).
17 D. Gittens, *The Family in Question* (Macmillan, 1985).
18 General Synod, 'Youth a Part?' (Church House Publishing, 1996) and Furnham.
19 C. New and M. David, *For the Children's Sake: Making childcare more than women's business* (Pelican, 1985).
20 R. McLoughry, *Men and Masculinity* (Hodder, 1992).
21 U. King, *Women and Spirituality: Voices of protest and promise* (Macmillan, 1993).
22 D. B. Gold, 'Women and Voluntarism', in V. Gornke, *Woman in Sexist Society* (Basic Books, 1971) and A. K. Daniels, *Invisible Careers* (University of Chicago Press, 1988).
23 A. J. Mills and S. J. Murgatroyd, *Organisational Rules* (Open University Press, 1991) and C. Itzin and J. Newman (Eds), *Gender, Culture and Organisational Change* (Routledge, 1995).
24 J. Lybeck and C. J. Neal, 'Do religious institutions resist or support women's "lost voice"?', *Youth and Society*, Vol. 27, No. 1, September 1995, pp. 4–25.
25 C. Gilligan, *In a Different Voice* (Harvard University Press, 1982).
26 H. O'Connell, *Women and the Family* (Zed Books, 1995).
27 Gill.
28 P. Leach, *Children First* (Michael Joseph, 1994) and R. Miles, *The Children we Deserve* (HarperCollins, 1994).

Chapter 9

1 These categories are derived from E. Eisner, *The Educational Imagination* (Macmillan, 1979).
2 On male contempt for females, see M. Sadker and D. Sadker, *Failing at Fairness* (Charles Scribner's Sons, 1994).
3 The classic account of this social construct of 'adolescence' is J. Kett, *Rites of Passage: Adolescence in America 1790 to present* (Basic Books, 1977). A comprehensive description of how youth culture is related to the emergence of modern mass media is Q. J. Schultze, *et al.*, *Dancing in the*

Dark: Youth popular culture and the electronic media (Eerdmans, 1991). A concise summary of these themes is found in R. R. Osmer, *Confirmation* (Geneva Press, 1996), pp. 3–26.

4 J. Fowler, *Becoming Adult, Becoming Christian* (Harper & Row, 1984).

5 P. Berger, *The Heretical Imperative: Contemporary possibilities of religious affirmation* (Anchor Press, 1979).

6 E. Erikson, *Identity, Youth and Crisis* (Norton, 1968).

7 Osmer, p. 15.

8 Schultze, *et al.*

9 L. Hardy, *The Fabric of This World* (Eerdmans, 1990), p. 48.

10 See Thomas G. Long's incisive discussion of a contemporary parable: 'Beavis and Butthead Get Saved', *Theology Today*, Vol. 51, No. 2, July 1994, pp. 199–203.

11 S. Hauerwas and W. Willimon, *Resident Aliens: Life in the Christian colony* (Abingdon, 1989).

12 K. Barth, *Church Dogmatics*, Vol. III, No. 4 (T. & T. Clark, 1961), p. 609. (Pronoun changes mine.)

13 Dorothy Bass (Ed.), *Practicing Our Faith: A way of life for a searching people* (Jossey-Bass, 1997), p. 5.

14 See L. P. Daloz, *et al.*, *Common Fire: Lives of commitment in a complex world* (Beacon Press, 1996).

15 Daloz, *et al.*, p. 64.

16 Daloz, *et al.*, p. 215.

17 The Youth Theology Institute is currently funded by a renewable grant from the Lilly Endowment to the Candler School of Theology at Emory.

18 A. N. Whitehead, *The Aims of Education* (Macmillan, 1929), pp. 15–28. One of the chief impediments to graduate theological education today is the loss of a romance phase with theological disciplines. Eager for seminarians to learn the grammar of their respective disciplines, instructors either presume or ignore the relational dynamics between students and subject matter. This rush towards precision and generalization is understandable within the context of curricular fragmentation, yet it does not serve the learning needs of students, who remain disconnected from what they are expected to know for the exam. Whitehead notes that 'a stage of precision is barren without a previous stage of romance.' Unless there are facts that have already been apprehended in their broad generality, the analysis of precision 'is simply a series of meaningless statements about bare facts, produced artificially and without any further relevance' (p. 18).

19 A year after his YTI experience, one alumnus remarked, 'My church youth group back home has these T-shirts that say "100% Catholic", and I can't wear that T-shirt because I can't say that I'm 100 per cent

Catholic any more. I'm like part Baptist, part Presbyterian, part . . . you know, a little bit of everything after YTI. So it's kind of given me, where, you know, you can look at all different perspectives, and see that whatever religious background you came from, it's not the only one.'

20 M. Belenky, B. Clinchy, N. Goldberger and J. Tarule, *Women's Ways of Knowing* (Basic Books, 1986). Belenky and her associates identify two modes of 'procedural knowing'. The 'separate' mode emphasizes objective reasoning, judgement by impersonal standards, a hermeneutics of suspicion. The 'connected' mode emphasizes conversation, empathy and understanding, a hermeneutics of generosity. Both separate and connected knowers 'learn to get out from behind their own eyes and use a different lens, in one case [separate] the lens of a disciple, in the other [connected] the lens of another person' (p. 115).

21 R. Kegan, *The Evolving Self* (Harvard University Press, 1982), pp. 25–45.

22 Kegan, pp. 121–32.

23 This alienation from the familiar is akin to that of the 'homecomer', as described by the sociologist Alfred Schutz in his *Collected Papers*, 3 Vols (Nijhoff, 1964), pp. 106–16.

24 James Keen is one of the co-authors of *Common Fire,* cited above. Keen and his wife, Cheryl, were the founding directors of the New Jersey Governor's School of Public Issues, a programme that provided the pedagogical model for YTI.

25 W. A. Visser and 't Hooft, 'The Word "Ecumenical" – Its History and Use', in R. Rouse and S. C. Neill (Eds), *A History of the Ecumenical Movement*, Vol. 1, 3rd edition (World Council of Churches, 1986), pp. 735–40.

26 See J. R. Nichols, 'Worship as Anti-structure: The contribution of Victor Turner', *Theology Today*, Vol. XLI, No. 4, January 1985, pp. 401–9.

27 D. Willis, *Daring Prayer* (John Knox Press, 1977), p. 57.

Chapter 10

1 G. Turner, *Film as Social Practice* (Routledge, 1993) p. 22.

2 S. Frith, *Music for Pleasure* (Routledge, 1988), p. 1.

3 *Newsweek*, 5 May, 1967, p. 61, quoted in Q. J. Schultze, *et al.*, *Dancing in the Dark: Youth popular culture and the electronic media* (Eerdmans, 1991), p. 217.

4 G. Melly, *Revolt into Style* (Allen Lane, 1970), p. 186.

5 H. Jenkins, quoted in J. Hollows and M. Jancovich (Eds), *Approaches to Popular Film* (Manchester University Press, 1995).

6 T. Schatz, 'The New Hollywood', in J. Collins, *et al.*, *Film Theory Goes to the Movies* (Routledge, 1993).
7 M. McLuhan, *Understanding Media* (McGraw-Hill, 1964).
8 D. F. Wells, *Whatever Happened to Truth?* (Eerdmans, 1993), pp. 89 and 90.
9 Wells, p. 75.
10 L. Mulvey, 'Visual pleasure and narrative cinema', *Screen 16*, No. 3, 1975.
11 Quoted in J. Williamson, *Consuming Passions: The dynamics of popular culture* (M. Boyars, 1988), p. 156.
12 N. Postman, *Technopoly* (Knopf, 1992).
13 Williamson, p. 199.
14 Turner, p. 112.
15 A. Toffler, *The Third Wave* (Morrow, 1980), p. 177.
16 Turner, p. 2.
17 Burchill, *Damaged Goods* (Century, 1986), pp. 137–8.
18 E. W. Said, *Culture and Imperialism* (Knopf, 1993), p. xxi.
19 M. Medved, 'Hollywood's Three Big Lies About Media and Society', speech to an Independent Policy Forum luncheon, San Francisco, 9 December, 1993.
20 G. E. Veith, *Guide to Contemporary Culture* (Word, 1994), pp. 124–5.